RAVE REVIEWS FOR KILLER QUESTIONS!

"Really enjoyed Killer Questions. It was like taking a peek into the minds of some of the greatest innovators in history right as they were asking these killer questions that prompted them to create history!"
—Kapil Kane, Head of R&D, **Intel China.**

"Awesome! It's a great book, I'm a huge fan of the power of questions."
—Peter Williams, VP, **Citibank.**

"Killer Questions is a Killer Book! This has really helped with both my classroom sessions and consulting projects. Good questions stimulate good answers. Well done!"
—James Reinnoldt, Adj. Professor, **The University of Washington.**

"More stimulating than a double shot of cold brew infused coffee. It is full of energy, fresh bright ideas, and reminds you how something you think is already well explored has room to grow even more. Now I can hand new engineers a strong cup of 'pure Stu' to kick-start their thinking. Make mine a double!"
—David Fincher, Fellow, **AMD.**

"Excellent information in a short time, thank you."
—Dr Friedrich Selles, R&D Director, **Siemens.**

"Stu is a rare "intellectual-doer" who boils ideas and insights down into digestible, actionable points that we can apply immediately to make us more effective, efficient and impactful. Stu is a guide who facilitates understanding, motivates, and ultimately helps us be better at our work."
—Will Nealy, Senior Manager, **adidas America.**

*Please leave a kind word for #killerquestions
on amazon.com or stulloyd.com*

KILLER QUESTIONS

How to shape better questions
that create explosive breakthroughs.

Stu Lloyd.

hotheadhacks
FUTURE SKILLS SERIES >>

Boring Stuff about the Publisher

The Hothead Hacks Future Skills Series is published by
Hotheads Innovation (HK) Ltd.
7F Kong Ling Building
100 Jervois Road
Sheung Wan
Hong Kong

Cover design: Stu Lloyd with Tatlin, DesignCrowd.com

Print book ISBN: 978-0-6481717-0-6
e-book ISBN: 978-0-6481717-2-0

Please enquire about bulk orders and special discounts for corporate orders.

All enquiries to mam@hotheads-innovation.com
www.hotheads-innovation.com

*"The important and difficult job is to find the right question.
There are few things as useless
– if not dangerous –
as the right answer to the wrong question."*

– Peter Drucker.

"Boring, bonehead questions are not cool."

– Elon Musk.

THANKS FOR ASKING

TO NONTHAPUN, MY ever-curious soul mate who asks as many questions as I do. Thanks for helping to compile all of this research. I hope this book answers why that needed to be done.

To my early manuscript readers:

Jim Reinnoldt at University of Washington, who was my client over 20 years ago and remains a great sparring partner.

Kapil Kane, who heads up Intel's R&D department in China and regales me with tales of working behind the black curtain at Apple.

David Fincher, a very fine Fellow at Advanced Micro Devices who once explained to me how the transistor radio works. And I got it. Sort of.

Peter Williams, who -- apart from playing the drums -- does clever things with the treasury at Citibank. 'Banker with a twist' is his self-styling.

Will Nealy, who gets a rush from developing his high performance teams at adidas and is one of the most active listeners I know.

You guys have no idea how daunting it was to humbly submit my System for your esteemed approval, comments and feedback. And how relieved I was when you gave it the thumbs up!

Thanks also to Tim Balbirnie, the irrepressible imaginator and predictor, and Rattaya Kulpradith, who generously volunteered corrections to my typos and oversights.

All those clients and thousands of workshop participants who helped shape this system, question by question, flipchart by flipchart, confirming to me that this was valuable stuff for you.

And especially to all the curious creators, those souls over the millennia who dared to ask Killer Questions that changed the world as we know it.

Without you, we'd all still be living in a cave in Ethiopia somewhere.

On second thoughts, what if we all still lived in a cave in Ethiopia somewhere?

CONTENTS

PACING THE FLOORBOARDS

Recently, I found myself in the uber-charming medieval city of Berne, Switzerland. One of its many attractions is a visit to the former family home of a young patent clerk, one Albert Einstein, who spent several years living in a rather modest walk-up apartment in the centre of the well-preserved old town.

Rather like the Marie-Celeste, I got the feeling of having just missed Einstein, with everything pretty much left as it was in his day. Perhaps he'd just stepped out for a walk? There's their baby bassinet. And, most inspiringly, the very desk from his time when he labored at the Patent Office.

And it was on these dark, creaking floorboards that Einstein would often pace, pondering issues of relativity. Back and forth, back and forth, repeating loudly to himself:

"If only I had the right question ...
If only I had the right question ... "

Because Einstein knew that having the right question would unlock the answers to the physical universe for him.

And pacing those floorboards was where suddenly everything unraveled to reveal E=MC2 as the answer (not 42, as many fans of *Hitchhikers Guide to the Galaxy* believe. That was the answer to the Ultimate Question of Life, the Universe and Everything.)

Another story involving Einstein has it that he was once being interviewed by the media, and the journalist asked him: "Mr Einstein, if a huge flaming meteor was on a collision course with the Earth, and you only had one hour to live, what would you do?"

Einstein wrinkled up his face, scratched his head, then apparently responded, "I would spend 55 minutes defining the problem, and 5 minutes solving it."

This, more than anything, underscores the importance he – as one of the world's foremost thinkers and problem solvers – put on getting the question right, and defining the challenge in just the right terms to fully understand it.

The inventor of the polio vaccine, Dr Jonas Salk, also saw it the same way. According to Salk:

> ***"You don't find the answers.***
> ***You reveal the answers by finding the right question."***

Almost channeling Salk here is the Danish convention-defying architect, Bjarke Ingels, shows us the way forward here, taking a customer-centric approach to understanding what their dreams, desires, and priorities might be. Then using that understanding as a creative springboard and driving force for his work. "Because the second we know what questions are important then all we have to do is answer them."

But here's the problem with that problem ...

Problem solving expert Thomas Wedell-Wedellsborg tells us that 85% of leading executives agree that their organizations are bad at problem diagnosis.

"What they struggle with," says Wedell-Wedellsborg in *Harvard Business Review*, "it turns out, is not solving problems but figuring out what the problems are."

Jim Reinnoldt, a lecturer in the International Business program at University of Washington, tells me: "Critical Questioning is not a skill that is promoted or developed in B-Schools. There's not enough focus on how you ask questions in the context of business." Although recently I spotted an ad for Monash University in Australia with the headline: "It's not what you know. It's what you question." So maybe there's hope.

Taking one step further back, questioning is often not encouraged (let alone taught as a skill) in schools.

Problem solving for many is not so much being a deer in the headlights. It's more like staring at the sun. We get so blinded we cannot see the blue sky all around it.

Researchers David G Jansson and Steven M Smith, from Texas A&M University, cracked their heads long and hard on this issue, and concluded:

"Thinking about problems first makes us 17 x more likely to fail."

In their corner is Morgan D. Jones, a US Army and CIA veteran, who has served as chief of that agency's analytic training branch. In his book *The Thinker's Toolkit* he tells us, "The moment we define a problem, our thinking about it narrows considerably."

To overcome such mental myopia, or tunnel vision, visual perception expert Amy Herman, advises us to "Look in a different direction, look to the edges, take a break from your current activity, and step back to make sure you're seeing the whole picture."

Focusing on *solutions* seems counter-intuitive: because most of our life's lessons are about focusing on a problem, working harder at it, digging deeper, throwing more resources at it, crawling deeper inside our problems with a negative, threat-analysis mindset.

But problems are often artificial barriers to us because we focus on the hole, not the donut. Like the 4-minute mile before Roger Bannister smashed it (then suddenly just about everyone with two legs could do it). Or, the Sub-2-Hour Marathon.

We need to adopt a positive and optimistic mindset about upside promotion and opportunity – an appreciative, growth mindset, not focus on downside prevention.

By setting our problems aside and seeking solutions, we can succeed beyond limitations, and have a much larger accomplishment than just solving that original perceived hurdle.

I call it Opportunity Creation Thinking. It's different from Problem Solving. It's Problem *Finding*. Finding a different, *better*, problem to solve.

WHAT IS A KILLER QUESTION?
A Killer Question is one with a unique perspective that sparks explosive insights and compels you to solve it creatively.

SO HOW DO WE GET FROM HERE TO THERE?
Thankfully, just after I had the Einstein experience (I was hoping for some brilliance to rub off by osmosis, but no), I came across the unstinting work of The Right Question Institute (yes, such a thing exists), and then the most exceptional book *A More Beautiful Question* by Warren Berger was published.

All these things collided in my mind with the work I had on my plate at that time with companies struggling for new ways to Find the Future.

I urge and commend (if not *command*) you to read Berger's book.

In it, he studied the greatest thinkers, inventors, innovators and entrepreneurs, from Leonardo da Vinci forward to this week's flavor-of-the-week Silicon Valley app developers and found that they all followed a certain pattern of inquiry.

THE BOTTOM LINE IS THIS DECEPTIVELY SIMPLE 3-STEP FORMULA:

1/ THEY START WITH A WHY QUESTION

2/ THEN TRANSFORM IT INTO A WHAT IF QUESTION

3/ WHICH THEN TURNS INTO A HOW QUESTION

And, voila, the solution is generally arrived at by tackling that last question. (See Chapter 4 for a fully worked example.)

In its simplest form, the Why question is a penetrative question which challenges the status quo, the accepted norm.

The What If question takes a creative leap forward by querying what might result if we looked at that problem differently, or reframed it to explore other possibilities.

Then the How question has the function of being the stepping-off point for us to brainstorm the solution and make that possibility into a reality.

The point is made that of course there can be some toggling and cycling, from, say, a What If question back to the Why stage. Or from How back to What if?

Now, if you're really lucky (and diligent and observant) a Killer Why question might – out of sheer curiosity – just present itself, then you are off to the races.

But What If you don't have that luck, and despite your challenging or curious mind, you don't have a Killer Question with which to kick start your innovation thinking and challenging process?

Aha – that's where KILLER QUESTIONS charges to the rescue, riding on the back of my own curiosity and desire to help others solve problems with bigger, hairier game-changing and genre-defining explosive ideas.

Because I start the process one key step earlier ... and end it a few steps later.

In my work with many brilliant individuals and teams at Fortune 500s there were folks experiencing exactly this dilemma. Wedded to the status quo. Or stuck in a rigid thought path borne of deep domain dominant logic. The paradox of experience.

SO HOW TO BREAK THE CAGE, JUMP THE RAILS, AND DISRUPT?

In this book I have codified and systemized what I call the KILLER QUESTIONS Innovation Question Formulation System. (Sorry, marketing department, there's no catchy acronym.)

Feel free to use and adapt any of the questions in this book for your own purposes. To spur you on to greater heights by thinking in questions. To shoot the lights out. To change the world. Like Richard Branson did ...

"In Virgin's early days, I would ask simple questions that others did not. Over the years, asking the simple questions and striving to answer them have become some of Virgin's most important characteristics."

Because if ideas are the currency of the New Economy, Killer Questions are the Bitcoin of the New Economy.

IT'S ABOUT YOUR BLINDSPOTS

My very modest background in psychology has grown wings over the years to the point now where it's a raging, passionate inferno of fascination with applied thinking, and all the sexy research that is now being done in the area of creative cognition.

And the big stumbling block is this:

WE ALL HAVE BLIND SPOTS.
AND WE ARE BLIND TO OUR BLIND SPOTS.

All experts, all experienced professionals, and especially all big and successful companies, are unknowingly carrying around excess baggage.

This "Corporate Cargo" are all the factoids we carry forward in our industry. Assumptions, assumed truths, invisible laws. The weight of history. The way things have always been done. Or the way things are still done around here.

This creates the blind spots which result in companies stumbling blindly forward in the darkness of blissful ignorance of the changed rules of the New Economy.

"All plans are based on assumptions," says author of *Red Teaming*, Bryce G. Hoffman. "All assumptions are based on understanding, and that understanding is frequently limited and often flawed. Too often assumptions are nothing more than wishful thinking."

I liken questions to a flashlight which shine light into the darkness of the unknown. Jeff Bezos calls them "blind alleys." By asking the right question, we surface more unknowns, learn, and gain greater strategic certainty.

This is doubly the case in these turbulent times.

"In the Old Economy, it was all about the answers. But in today's dynamic, lean economy it's more about asking the right questions," **advises Eric Ries, the man who kick-started** *The Lean Startup* **revolution.**

One thing I know for sure is that in my 30 years at the intersection of creativity and commerce, I have often come up with brilliant answers (if I may say so myself) to the completely wrong question. Absolutely freaking useless! No value to anyone!

Because the brief, or the problem definition, was not given enough thought. All the effort and focus was put on generating a clever creative solution. And not enough on really nailing the nature of the problem or opportunity. Think of it as a misguided missile.

It's like a tee shot on the golf course. If you're a little out at the point of impact, you are massively wrong by the time the ball lands in the water or sand or trees way off to the left somewhere. Trust me, I know a lot about that.

THE KILLER
QUESTIONS CANVAS

THE KILLER QUESTIONS
(INNOVATION QUESTION FORMULATION) SYSTEM
STEP-BY-STEP CANVAS

1/ Thinking Focus. Area or Problem? Are you just having blue sky/ greenfield opportunity ideas for a certain domain, or is there a particular problem/challenge to address? Write it at the top of the page to keep yourself on task.

FOCUS:

2/ Assumption Dump. Let's expose Blind Spots and list all the things we take for granted, all the things that our product or solution "must" be or must have. Think in terms of materials, size, shape, and parts, etc. Make them as dumb and obvious and broad as possible.

ASSUMPTIONS:

3/ Why Questions. Add the word 'Why?' in front of your assumptions to make them penetrating Why questions. We zoom out, step back and look at the real fundamentals. Make all questions open-ended.

WHY?

4/ What If Questions. We take a creative leap. We twist it by reversing our Why questions, turning them upside down, stretching them by adding a zero, or two 00s, or three 000s. Or squeeze them by making them smaller. Much much smaller.

WHAT IF?

5/ How Might We Questions. Format: How Might We (achieve our objective)? We're trying to craft the perfect springboard question to brainstorm on here.

HOW MIGHT WE?

6/ Harvest and Prioritise Question/s. Which is the most INTERESTING question to answer? Which is the most URGENT question to answer? Which is the most IMPORTANT question to answer? A simple group voting with red sticky dots works great, but don't follow the herd or the leader. Use your OWN judgment.

7/ Improve your Selected Question/s. Can you tweak the verb to add energy? Can you make it more general or more specific? Can you change the perspective of who's asking the question? Can it be broken down further to zoom into a particular part of the question/ problem?

8/ Tadaa!!!

OUR KILLER QUESTION IS

—

9/ Now stick this question up somewhere for you and others to see it. Set timeline to sit down and brainstorm the Killer Solution.

Because **CREATIVITY +** *ACTION* **= INNOVATION.**

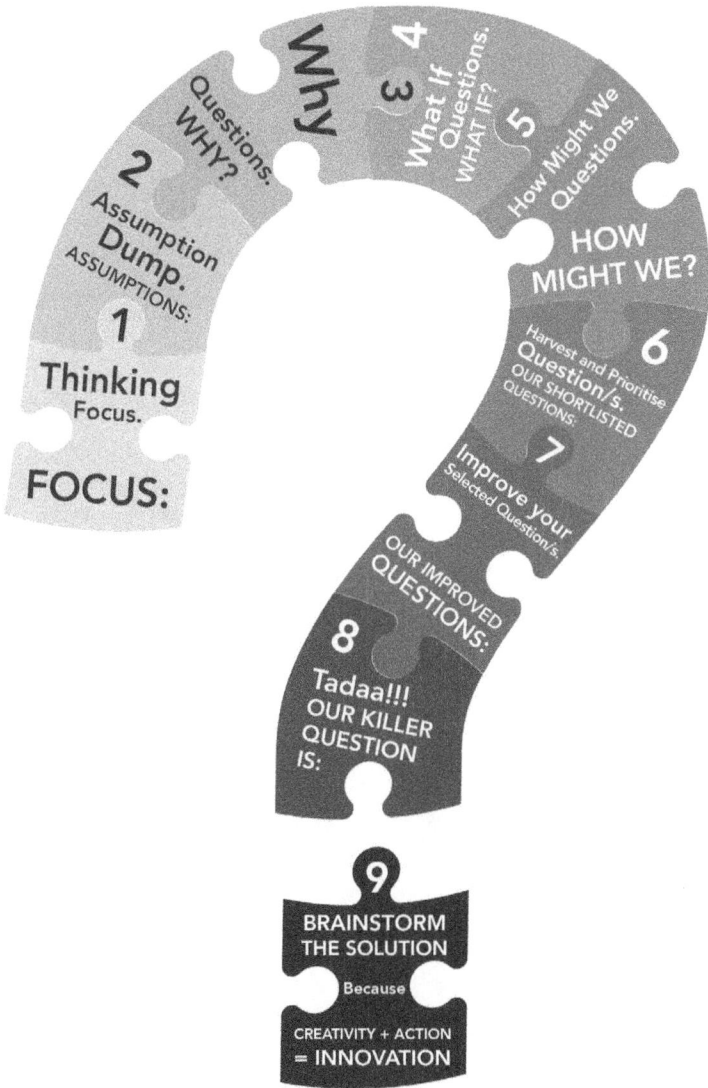

The Killer Questions Canvas (question-mark shaped puzzle):

1 — Thinking Focus. FOCUS:
2 — Assumption Dump. ASSUMPTIONS:
Questions. WHY?
Why
3 — What If Questions. WHAT IF?
4
5 — How Might We Questions. HOW MIGHT WE?
6 — Harvest and Prioritise Question/s. OUR SHORTLISTED QUESTIONS.
7 — Improve your Selected Question/s. OUR IMPROVED QUESTIONS:
8 — Tadaa!!! OUR KILLER QUESTION IS:
9 — BRAINSTORM THE SOLUTION. Because CREATIVITY + ACTION = INNOVATION

**Download this Canvas free from
www.hotheads-innovation.com/killerquestions**

A HANDS-ON EXAMPLE

L et's say we are Sir James Dyson and we've decided to turn our attention to redesigning the humble hand drying experience, as found in washrooms all around the world, a process unchanged and unloved and unthought about for the past few decades.

So, step 1, write your focus at the top of the page:

"Radically Improving the Hand Drying Experience."

This one's an Area focus. Use nice strong verbs to set the tone for energized thinking.

Step 2 is a data dump of assumptions about hand dryers.

The first big one is that the hand dryer "must have" paper towels or a roll of cloth towel. We can agree those are about the most basic truths of that thing, right?

So, we list that down, plus all the other things we can think of, such that it must be in a bathroom, it must be refilled, it must be washed and serviced, someone must come and check it periodically, etc.

Now let's plug this into the Killer Question formula ...

Next, Step 3, we turn those assumptions into Why? Questions.

So, it becomes:

"Why must we have a paper towel?" (Pause for derisive laughter)

And,

"Why must we have a roll of cloth?" (Again, knowing sniggers and sneers.)

"Why must it be in the bathroom?"

"Why must it be refilled?"

"Why must it be washed and serviced?"

"Why must someone come along to check it periodically?"

You get the idea. It doesn't have to be slavishly one-for-one in going from Assumptions to Why questions. If another question is sparked, or a subtle variation on one, great, write that down too. Keep the process, loose, and fluid and creative as possible.

Then we move to Step 4, the What If? stage.

This is where we enter the realm of unfettered fantastic possibility (I'll share with you how you do this in a later chapter, but for now we're just outlining the process.)

Dyson might then have thought to himself:

"What if we had no paper towel?"

Or,

"What if we had no cloth roll?"

Again, expect guffaws of "Haha! Crazy, of course you've gotta have a towel!"

As Linda Rottenberg eloquently put it in her book of the same name: Crazy is a Compliment. Amen to that!

In my experience the answer that elicits a laugh or a guffaw is probably the solution we should examine most closely for potential because that's the one with the most crazy creative energy. People laugh and reject it out of hand because it does not fit easily into a pre-assigned cookie-cutter hole in our brain. Because it's a brand new unrecognizable shape for now.

So the masses laugh out of nervous awkwardness, automatically rejecting it – because it's unfamiliarnot because it's necessarily a bad idea.

Here's the rule of thumb: if someone says straight off: "Oh, that's a good idea!" then no, it's not. What they really mean is, Oh that idea feels safe and comfortable because I could immediately slot it into a certain hole in my brain.

"If at the first the idea is not absurd, there is no hope for it."
Einstein.

"We all know your idea is crazy.
The question is, whether it is crazy enough?"
Niels Bohr, Nobel Prize-winning physicist.

"Good ideas are always crazy until they're not."
Larry Page, Google co-founder.

So we need to fully enjoy the playful absurdity of the What if? phase, accepting all seemingly improbable scenarios that your professional judgment is dying to reject and kill off.

Instead, push through it to the next step. Because remember, at this stage, we are only interested in creating the KILLER QUESTION that will lead us to the big idea. We are not looking for, nor interested in, the solution just yet. We're looking for questions, not answers.

And so we move to Step 5, the How? part of the process

At this point Dyson might then generate the following questions:

At this point Dyson might then generate the following questions:

"How can we have a hand dryer with no paper towel?"
Or,
"How could we design a hand dryer that doesn't use cloth roll?"

And so the dramatic stage is set.

How indeed?
Our beautiful restless super-computer brains would love to take this question away and work on it in the background. While you're working on some dull admin stuff, busy playing facebook, or taking a shower, exercising and especially sleeping, associative thinking automatically happens.
As we now know, the result of that challenge from Dyson, was the Air Jet, a completely revolutionary take on the hand dryer.
So, yes, it's that easy. Haha, don't we wish?

ASSUMPTIONS

- ☒ WE PRODUCE CHEMICALS
- WE NEED SALES PEOPLE
- WE NEED B✗✗
- WE ARE GLOBAL
- WE NEED PROFITS
- WE NEED HIGH MARGINS
- WE ARE TECHNICAL (GERMAN COMPANY)
- WE NEED CONTROLLED BUSINESS WORKS
- OUR PRODUCTS ARE COMMODITY
- PLEASE OUR CUSTOMERS
- ☒ STRATEGIC PLAN

WHY?

- WE DO WE PRODUCE CHEMICAL
- WE DO WE NEED SALES PEOPLE?
- WHY WE NEED B✗✗
- WHY DON'T WE BECOME INTRAPRENEURS
- WHY ARE WE GLOBAL?
- WHY WE NEED (SO MUCH) PROFITS
- WHY ARE OUR PRODUCTS SOLD FOR ????
- WHY WE NEED HIGH MARGINS
- WE ARE WE SO TECHNICAL
- WE DO WE NEED SO MANY CONTROLS
- WHY OUR PRODUCTS BECOME COMMO????
- WE WE NEED TO PLEASE OUR CUSTOMER
- WHY WE NEED STRATEGIC PLAN?

WHAT IF?

- WHAT IF WE CHANGE THE NAME?
- what if we don't produce chemical
- what if we trade chemicals?
- WI WE GO LOCAL?
- what if we fired all sales people
- what if sales people turn entrepreneurs
- what if we ~~donated~~ donate all profit?
- VI WE JV with ~~customer~~ donate
- what if we giveaway product for free
- what if we are not push on technical
- WI OUR PRODUCTS BUT WE CHARGE FOR SERVICE
- WI WE ARE LO-TECH?
- "... " SUPER HI TECH?
- WI WE ALSO NEED TO PLEASE OUR CUSTOMER'S CUSTOMERS
- WI WE MAKE CUSTOMERS LOVE US?
- WI WE HAVE NO BOSS
- WI WE CAN PRODUCE OTHER PRODUCTS?
- WI WE JUST DO IT

HMW:

- HMW CHANGE THE NAME?
- HMW CHANGE THE NAME
- HMW WE PRODUCE A SUBSTITUTE FOR ????
- HMW TRADE CHEMICALS
- HMW WE DO BUSINESS WITHOUT SALES
- HMW WE GROW WITHOUT SALESPEOPLE
- HMW WE GO LOCAL?
- HMW GROW WITHOUT BOSS
- HMW TURN SALES PEOPLE INTO INTRAPRENEURS?
- HMW SURVIVE WITHOUT PROFIT
  - HMW DIFFERENT FROM OUR DONATION
  - HMW CHARGE FOR OUR SERVICES
  - HMW GIVE OUR PRODUCTS AWAY + STILL MAKE PROFIT
  - HMW BECOME A MARKETING/&CO
  - " " DISTRIBUTION CO
- HMW MOVE MORE TOWARDS WITH LO/LOWER TECH PRODUCTS
- HMW GROW BUSINESS WITH OUR CUSTOMER?
- HMW PRODUCE OTHER PRODUCTS WITH CURRENT ????
- HMW DO BUSINESS WITHOUT A PLAN?
- HMW WE TRUST OUR EMPLOYEES?
- ☒ HMW JUST DO IT.
- HMW CHANGE CUSTOMER BEHAVIOUR

A MATTER OF FOCUS

Thinking Focii come in two flavours:

1/ Area Focus

2/ Problem Focus

The first is what I call "blue sky" or "green field" thinking. This is the sort of ideation brainstorm exercise in which you just want to do some wide open opportunity creation thinking.

For example, you're an entrepreneur who wants to drum up some fresh new ideas for a Mexican themed diner.

There's no particular problem to solve, nor looming deadline to avoid a crisis. Rather you're looking for a juicy problem to find.

We call this an Area focus. You're looking for ideas in this general Area.

Howard Schulz might have written "Ideas for Coffee Bars" at the top of his page in Step 1 when he was conceiving Starbucks.

The second type is a Problem Focus. It's not necessarily a "problem", as in something's gone wrong, but can be a challenge or situation that can be clearly defined and needs to be specifically addressed, to improve the effectiveness, or efficiency or uniqueness of that thing.

"**What are we *REALLY* trying to do here?**" asks Pierre Omidyar, founder of eBay, to get to the heart of the macro objective of anything. This might well be the kick-off question for you in Step 1 when you're considering your thinking focus. I capitalize and bold and italicize the word "*REALLY*" because it forces you to think beyond the lazy low-hanging fruit, beyond what Hamilton creator Lin Manuel Miranda calls the "rusty-water" first thoughts.

Advice from Dwayne Spradlin, CEO of high-calibre crowd-sourcing problem solving site, Innocentive.com, is to first articulate the problem in the simplest terms possible:

"WE ARE LOOKING FOR X IN ORDER TO ACHIEVE Z AS MEASURED BY W."

So you might want to start by writing that at the top of your page, as Step 1.

Example: P&G engineers in looking to improve Tide might say: "We are looking for a way to stop dirt binding with other garments in the washing machine to keep your colours pure."

"**A problem well-stated is a problem half-solved,**" famous educationalist and psychologist John Dewey told us.

The problem is that inexperienced and impatient problem solvers too often jump headfirst from that problem statement into brainstorming for solutions.

No, No, No ... and, again, NO!

STEP TWO

TAKING A DUMP

So how do we surface our blindspots? How do we identify what's in danger of derailing our thinking, or taking us down a marginal path of incremental progress?

WE DUMP OUR ASSUMPTIONS. MAKE A BIG LIST. ON A FLIPCHART, FOR ALL TO SEE.

What are the absolute must haves, fake truisms, givens, and "articles of faith" you are working with or considering each time you sit down to develop a new product, tweak a process, or solve a challenge?

(Some of these assumptions may turn out to be 'true facts' but they haven't been fully tested yet.)

Let me give you some examples from some recent client 'brainstorm' exercises.

Working with Citibank, we might start with something like "A bank must have branches."

Working with Accor, we might start with "A hotel must have hotel rooms."

Working with Pfizer, we might start with "A drug must have active ingredients."

Usually there are guffaws of "Of course!" from around the room, and especially the skeptics at the edges of the room.

The point here is to capture the most blindingly obvious, deep and broad assumptions possible.

What are the most established, unquestionable things? Question those.

And the deeper and broader they are, the more scope you have to turn your industry or category on its ear.

Often time the most obvious things – the great shiny thing right in front of their noses – is the thing they don't see. *Refrigerator blindness.* As in, "Honey, do we have any milk? I can't see it anywhere." I need to prompt them.

For example, a group of designers from a leading sports brand in one workshop completely neglected to mention that they had to include their striped logo on each and every piece of apparel and footwear.

If you're dealing with physical product design, give especial thought to materials, size, shape, and parts.

I like to fill a whole page with about 25 or more assumptions. Keep going. As many as you can squeeze out is good.

And so, in Step 2, all the assumptions are dumped onto a flipchart.

WHY? QUESTIONS

S ome of my most vivid memories of being a father of two young children involve family drives on a weekend, either down to the glittering golden beaches of Sydney's northern coast, or up into the Blue Mountains to the west.

These journeys seemed to be a catalyst for questions from Jasmine, then about 5 or 6 years old.

"Why are there waves in the sea, daddy?"

"Why are they called the Blue Mountains but they are green?"

"Why do seagulls like chips?"

I enjoyed fielding the easier questions, others forced me to really think things through. And then when she kept drilling deeper, with more successive Why questions, my head started to hurt with the thought given to things we – as boring, conditioned adults – just take as given in our surroundings.

We simply stop seeing. We get comfortably numb.

I thank my parents for blessing me with a curious mind, and I am glad I have passed this on to both my children, who read voraciously and have encyclopedic knowledge of so much.

Recent research outed the fact that the average child in the UK had asked around 40,000 questions by the time of their 6th birthday.

Kids are hungry and thirsty to download what they can of the world's knowledge, sponge-like, into their growing brains. They are also keen to make meaning of the otherwise random, orderless world.

But, then a curious thing happens ...

We go to school and get force-fed the answers. Some teachers take questioning as disruptive behavior not to be tolerated. Why? Because it just is. I said so, and I'm the teacher, so there. Which shuts us down further. Our rate of questioning dips.

Then we hit teenage-hood and a rebellious spirit kicks in. Why questions get replaced by Why Not questions, and then questions are suddenly replaced altogether by Because... statements in early adulthood.

If you were anything like me, you'll remember you were bullet-proof and knew everything by the age of twenty.

And this attitude carries along with most of us into the workplace, especially when it seems imperative to know everything if you're a professional manager.

The status quo absorbs us and welcomes us, as long as we go with the flow. The bureaucracy actually self-forms and bonds around the status quo, like an immune system, to protect it from invasive new ideas.

Making our big and successful ship as hard to turn as a super-tanker (which take tens of kilometers, and perhaps up to 30 minutes, to stop when needed).

Unfortunately the New Economy is asking for jet skis, able to zig and zag, turn on a dime, and explore exciting new sea routes to the New World of the future.

"Challenge convention," **advises edgy hotelier, Alex Calderwood, who heads up buzzy and trendy ACE Hotels.** *"Do not buy into the idea that things have to work the way they have in the past, nor operate the way the industry tells you they should."*

In this age of complexity, Warren Berger points out that answers – a fixed body of knowledge – have diminishing value, whereas questions are gaining in value.

And of all the questions, Why questions are possibly the most valuable.

Because they are explosive, exploratory, brazenly challenge the current situation.

When we ask Why questions (and yes, I include Why Not and Why Don't We … in the same vein) we are actually taking a step back. We are taking our noses out of the third decimal point of that Excel spreadsheet.

The world has become terribly accomplished, not to mention fixated, at zooming in. Because we can. Technology and Big Data has facilitated this. But our muscles for stepping back, zooming out and seeing the big picture, have atrophied.

It's a rare mind who can see and deal with such complexity. Your Jobs's and your Musk's are archetypal big picture eco-system thinkers. Able to zoom out, and then further out again, in order to see all the possible moving parts of an eco-system, and then using their advanced skills of complexity and associative thinking, to see how all those parts could be joined or smartly recombined to create a new or different whole.

Like iTunes. Or a re-usable space rocket.

So Why questions are the quickest and easiest way to Zoom Out and challenge the way things are done. Be it your whole industry, your business model, a new product design, or simply the leave application process in your office.

If you already come to the 'brainstorm' session with a Why question in mind, of course you should write it up on the flipchart (or the attached Canvas). And you can just include it among the other Why questions which will be formed around it.

Why questions cause us to Unlearn, to invoke the deliciously desirable Beginner's Mind state again.

SOME KILLER WHY? QUESTIONS.

Following are a bunch of great Why questions that have been let loose in the world by great thinkers, old and new, from many different sectors.

While many are verbatim quotes, some may have been inferred from the line of thinking or reverse-engineered from the subsequent action or result. But the challenging spirit of them cannot be denied.

Sometimes their very obviousness is the thing that makes them so powerful. Because they've questioned the unquestionable, and exposed a great big blindspot hiding in plain sight in front of our noses.

Other times, it is the nuanced semantics that creates the power of the line of enquiry.

Airlines:
"Why do air fares have to be so expensive?" wondered a young Malaysian, Tony Fernandes, as he sat at boarding school in England, feeling homesick and begudging the distance and cost that separated him from his beloved family. He answered this by founding Air Asia, voted the world's best low-cost carrier by SkyTrax several years in a row.

I'm old enough to remember when air tickets were little booklets of several pages with carbon sheets inside. If you lost that, that was it, buddy, you couldn't board your flight. Insane, thought, David Neeleman, founder of JetBlue. **"Why do we treat tickets like cash? Is there a better way?"** Yes.

Around the same time a global distribution study was being done, of which Jim Reinnoldt (now at University of Washington) was a part. "Someone asked, **"Why do we need paper tickets? They cost $12 to print, process and store. And people keep losing them?"** There was a pause in the room, and soon after we started looking at electronic tickets," he says.

The industry soon moved away from paper, developing a booking code, so a lost ticket could be traced and replaced using that. Which later led to the introduction of e-tickets. Enabling me now to arrive at the airport and plonk just my passport on the check-in counter to get on board.

Later, seeing that JetBlue's perky price promotions were not converting as many new customers as he'd like, Neeleman questioned: **"Why aren't more passengers taking advantage of our cheap fares?"** It turned out that the taxi fares to the airport were often more than the airfare itself, making it unaffordable. So JetBlue set up a fleet of buses offering free shuttles to the airport. That did the trick, and JetBlue was one of only very few airlines that posted profits in the post 9-11 era.

A more controversial and spiky question occurred to Michael O'Leary, the fast and often loose-talking CEO of low-cost carrier, Ryan Air: **"Why do we need travel agents?"** The answer was, actually, they didn't. The rest – almost like travel agents themselves – is history, and savings of multiple millions of dollars were ushered in for the airline industry.

Banking/ Finance:

A Scottish inventor, John Shepherd-Barron, was sitting in his bathtub when he had a flash of inspiration: **"If vending machines can dispense chocolate bars, why couldn't they dispense cash?"** He sold his idea to Barclay's Bank in 1967, and soon after the first ATM made its debut.

"Why should it take a week to replace an ATM card?" asked former CEO of Commerce Bank, Vernon Hill. (With lines of questioning like that, he's a guy I could really like.) "It's nuts," he said, "we're in the convenience business." Instead of mailing an application form and going through all that tedious crap, he made his bank issue replacement cards that were activated in-store on the spot. No wonder Commerce Bank out-performed the industry, growing their deposit base by 25% annually (compared to industry average of just 5%) and delivering a 23% annual shareholder return every year for 30 years. This one really resonates with me, having been just told by my bank, I must appear in person at my original bank branch – in a city 1000km away – in order to replace my card which their faulty ATM machine just swallowed. Yes, a true story from 2017. Medieval dullards!

Medical.

"Why don't milkmaids get smallpox?" was a question that plagued (sorry!) Edward Jenner, sharply noticing that in outbreaks which killed up to 35% of populations, milkmaids never got it, nor died from it. He followed up his observation that milkmaids who had previously caught cowpox did not later catch smallpox, by showing that inoculated cowpox protected against inoculated smallpox.

Van Philips is an amputee, and was struggling with his artificial leg, which was like prosthetics of old: clunky and a poor imitation of an actual leg and foot. This caused him great discomfort and the occasional fall flat on his face. **"If they can put a man on the moon,"** he thought, **"Why they can't they make a decent foot?"** This set him on an iterative journey which resulted in the curved Cheetah blades (made famous by amputee Olympian-turned girlfriend killer Oscar 'Blade Runner' Pistorius).

"Why aren't people in developing countries using the incubators they have?" is the question that came to Jane Chen, who was on an assignment set by Stanford to redesign the incubator. Following this line of enquiry led her to discover that many remote clinics had no electricity, and no funds for maintenance. This led her to design the Embrace incubator, powered by boiling water, and costing just $25 compared to $20,000. An estimated 200,000 babies have been saved already. Bravo, Jane!

Jake Andraka was, by all accounts, a very ordinary student, muddling his way through high school (boy, can I relate to that!) But when his uncle died of pancreatic cancer, it was a sad blow for Jake. His parents outlined why pancreatic cancer was such a devastating killer that many didn't test for until it was way too late because of the $800 price tag. **"Why are we so bad at detecting pancreatic cancer? Why isn't there a fast, inexpensive test for pancreatic cancer?"** Jake asked and set about answering. The result? This 15 year old created, pretty much on his own, with some help from the labs at Johns Hopkins University, a new test for pancreatic cancer which came in at 3 cents per time (1/26,000th the cost), with 25-50% greater accuracy and 168 times the speed. Truly awesome example of beginner's mind combining with curiosity and persistence.

Entertainment.

Walt Disney was an 'always on' thinker, and a great cross-pollinator. So the question struck him when he was obviously a little bored on a family outing to a local theme park for children. **"Why isn't there any entertainment here for parents?"** Taking that to its extreme could've resulted in something like Bangkok's notorious Patpong or Soi Cowboy bar districts, but instead sparked the idea for Disneyland.

"Why do interactions between humans and aliens have to be antagonistic?" This question helped Steven Spielberg to meet his objective of bucking the trend in extraterrestrial movies to date. He didn't understand why an alien coming all the way to earth would necessarily want to be confrontational. This different depiction became *Close Encounters of the Third Kind*, which grossed over $300,000,000 dollars on a $20,000,000 production budget.

The famed Japanese director Akira Kurosawa, reflected back on his body of work (*Seven Samurai, Kagemusha*, etc), and discovered something surprising even to himself: "I suppose all my films have a common theme. If I think about though, the only theme is a question: **Why can't people be happier together?"**

"Why do we have to follow the same formula? Why can't you take a punt?" was the driving question that Tahir Bilgic, an Australian comedian, asked of himself and TV executives. (A punt means a gamble.) The result was the smash comedy show *Here Come the Habibs* which has brought a Middle Eastern family sitcom into the prime time lounge rooms of Australia.

"Fuck it. Why don't I do the most complex record that I've ever done?" is how Neil Finn – former Split Enz and Crowded House frontman – challenged himself on his latest 'solo' album. "I could have done a little acoustic album live on the internet, that would've been easy." Instead he wheeled in a 30-piece orchestra and choir ensemble, and live-streamed rehearsals and recording to facebook, launching a fully mixed album *Out of Silence* within days of that.

Media.

"Why do we tell the stories we tell, the way we tell them?" is what drove Joseph Campbell in 1949 to investigate and finally proscribe his story arc of the Hero's Journey ... that same storyline that carries through everything from the Bible to *The Lord of the Rings* to the *Matrix* to *Harry Potter* to *Star Wars*. Read his book *Hero of a Thousand Faces* to learn the intricacies of this theory.

"Why do people share what they share? is to ask What connects people?" asks Derek Thompson in his book, *Hit Makers*. He quotes Stanford research which shows that we should think beyond just your friends and followers, but to the audience of your audience. So I should ask you – who are you going to share the ideas in this book with? (Use hashtag #killerquestions.)

Sport.

Wayne Gretzky has outperformed any other ice hockey player on just about every metric you can think of. A challenging question always on his mind was: **"If it's legal, why not?"** This led to his never-tried-before move of flicking the puck up from behind the goal, over the net, for a teammate to tap it in from the front, leaving the opposition goalkeeper blindsided and bewildered. (Paraphrased: Why the puck not???)

Dwayne Douglas was the beleaguered coach of the Florida Gators. His football team was not performing well. As he watched them sweltering at training and on match days in the tropical Floridian heat, he made an observation. No one seemed to need a pee. **"Why aren't our players urinating more often?"** he asked. Of course it was dehydration. So he set about mixing up some sugars and salts in water to replenish them. That did the trick! Gatorade was born, his team won the following year's championship, and a $20 billion sports drink industry was born.

Religion.

"Why does 1 in 1000 people become radicalized?" is what British MP Anne Aly has been wondering lately, in the wake of increased home grown terrorism in the UK.

"Why should we limit the learning that pastors and faith-based leaders are exposed to?" wondered Bill Hybels, founder of Willow Creek Church, one of the largest and fastest growing in the USA. That question led to the creation of the Willow Creek Global Leadership Summit, which attracts some 7000 faith-based leaders, who get to hear the likes of GE's Jack Welch, Colin Powell, and Jim Collins speaking in a power-packed program.

E-commerce.

Australian doctor-turned-online entrepreneur, Dr Matt Schiller was working on one of his businesses, GownTown, that country's largest online graduation retailer, when he had an epiphany. "We offered photography along with academic dress, which proved popular with customers. That got us thinking, **"Why aren't we doing this for *all* photography?"** This insight led to developing Snappr, the "Uber for photography." The app makes quality photography more accessible to consumers, connecting them with pre-vetted photographers from less than $50.

A group of cash-poor students sat around the table, bemoaning the state of their spectacles, and wishing they could repair or replace their glasses, which had sticky-tape holding bits together. **"Why does such a fundamentally simple product cost more than a smartphone?"** they wondered. This challenging question animated the group into further discussion of a cut-price optical service. Online. It became known as Warby Parker, disrupted the eyewear industry as we know it, and currently enjoys a market valuation of $1.2 billion. I bet no one saw that coming.

Food.

Caleb Harper is an "aircologist" who works at MIT Media Labs, and was recognized by Nat Geo as one of its Emerging Explorers in 2015. On the subject of food transportation, he's been wrestling with a question: **"Why can't we atomise food and reconstitute it on the other side?"**

"Why isn't there a high-quality coffee equivalent to the common tea bag?" was the question that came to John Sylvan. This led to him developing the Keurig single-cup coffee capsule system, which replaced the big old pots of stale coffee which most companies had sitting around. Keurig jagged nearly 20% of the corporate coffee market, became a billion-dollar brand, and sold out to Green Mountain Coffee Roasters.

You'd think the world already had enough burger and fried chicken joints. But Adam Fleischman didn't think so, and set up Umami Burger in 2009 to "amplify your taste buds" with a fifth flavor sense, umami. One day he received a call at his office from a guy who said he had an amazing chocolate chicken recipe to share. Most CEO's would've probably slammed the phone down on a suspected prank caller at that stage, but Fleischman set up a meeting, and heard out the guy's idea.

"Hey, why don't we take fried chicken and turn it on its ear?" enthused Fleischman. The result was the ChocoChicken Restaurant in LA. "Most addicting meal I ever had!" enthused one punter on TripAdvisor, but sadly – and perhaps not surprisingly to many – the restaurant has now closed. A rare example of a failure in this book.

Former soda marketer Jeffrey Dunn came on board at Bolthouse Farms, with a question gnawing at him: **"If Coca Cola could persuade people to drink more than a billion servings of its soda each day, why couldn't we do the same for a vegetable?"** This got him thinking of using junk food marketing tactics for his company's healthy stuff like carrot snack packs, a really disruptive approach resulting in selling through vending machines, licensing Sesame Street characters and selling through 7-Eleven.

Apropos of nothing at all, Peter Fitzsimons, former Wallaby rugby player and columnist for the *Sydney Morning Herald*, asks: **"Why does a round pizza come in a square box?"** and **"Why do toasters always have a setting that burns the toast to a horrible crisp that no decent human being would eat?"**

Hospitality.

As the TV News broadcast the chaos and congestion of a huge convention in their town, leaving many attendees without hotel accommodation, three struggling tech students sat around their kitchen table wondering how they could cobble together that month's rent. **"Why should they be stuck without a bed, if we've got extra room space here? Why can't they find a place to crash for a night or two? Why not *our* place?"** someone, possibly Joe Gebbia, asked.

The question sparked the idea to run down to Walmart, buy some air mattresses, some Coco Pops, and hack together a website quickly. They then alerted the local news channel that Air Bed & Breakfast (later rebranded AirB&B) was open for business. CNN soon picked up and amplified that gutsy story, and we now know that those guys are not struggling to pay the rent anymore.

"Why do people want to work with us?" asks Daniel Humm, founder of Eleven Madison Park, voted the world's top restaurant in 2017. Although he sees his restaurant as a leader, they are always learning. "If people want to work with us we give them an education. I think as much as how to motivate them as what goes on the plate." If only more employers thought like this.

Global CMO at Hilton Hotels, Geraldine Calpin, looked at airline websites and your ability to customize your seating arrangements and other opt-in opt-out services. **"Why can't our guests have the same level of personalization at our hotels, like on an airplane?"** she wondered. This cross-sectoral thinking led to Hilton importing the idea of digital floor plans which guests can select rooms from, and to date already 13,000,000 rooms have been selected and bought in this new way.

Retail.

Returning his family's rented copy of Apollo 13 one day, Reed Hastings grumbled: **"Why should I have to pay their late fees?"** Well, because you returned it late, Sir! But as he'd just come from the gym, it started the thought process of why a video store couldn't run on the same annual membership model. Whether you used it or not, it costs the same. And so the idea of Netflix was born. Good challenge, Sir!

"Why can't everyone accept credit cards?" pondered

Jack Dorsey, after his friend, a glasswork designer, had to forego a sale because a client could only pay with credit card and he wasn't a merchant. See how this thinking moved to the next level in the What If chapter ... which led to Square disrupting the payments industry.

University life.

Like many university students, Gauri Nanda had a problem at university. Not so much sleeping through lectures at MIT as much as sleeping in and missing them entirely. **"Why am I oversleeping – why isn't my alarm clock getting me up?"** Keep reading for her What If question that led to a student revolution ...

Humanity.

"If something can't hurt me, then why should it scare me?" was the question that set Jia Jiang off on the crazy series of escapades that resulted in his great book of transformative self-discovery, *Rejection Proof.* YouTube his videos. Funny stuff as he overcomes his fear of rejection and discovers self-confidence.

Leisure.

Dave Evans was an engineer at Gore, and loved to escape the stresses of that by mountain biking at the weekends. Except that came with its own stresses. **"Why can't I get the gears on my bike to shift more smoothly?"** This led down the path of plastic-coated cables to minimize rusting and metal-on-metal chafing. Gore launched the Ride-On gear cables to much acclaim and market share.

Office Products.

Bette Graham was working her humdrum typing job

in a local bank, with Christmas coming soon. She watched the window decorators at work, painting a festive message on the bank's window. She noticed that everytime they made a mistake, they just painted white over it, and re-did that bit again so it looked perfect. Hmm. **"Why can't I do that with my bad typing?"** she asked herself. She went home and mixed up some acrylic paint and water, and came back and tried it the next day. It worked! She could paint over her mistakes, and retype the sentence. She sold Tippex, her brand, to Gillette for $47.5m back when that was a shit-ton of money.

Architecture.

Kristen Whittle is one of Australia's, most progressive architects, who loves to blend the natural and social factors in his projects in Melbourne, often listed as the most liveable city in the world.

"Why can't our cities be as beautiful as nature and parks?" he likes to ask. **"Why can't architecture be as restorative to us as the sunset at a beach?"** This social-natural connection is informing a lot of his work, such as the 52-metre high timber "plyscraper" tower in King St, Brisbane, said to be the world's largest timber building.

Work culture.

Ricardo Semler, CEO of Brazilian megalith, Semco Partners is a huge fan of corporate democracy and living life while you're alive. So 30 years ago he started posing questions of the way companies, including his own, actually operated.

"Why do we want know what time you came to work, what time you left, etc. Can't we exchange for this for a contract for buying something from you?" He went further: **"Why can't people set their own salaries?"**

His company grew in 20 years from $4m turnover to

over $212m.

Another was on the issue of challenging corporate ego. **"Why are we building these headquarters?"** Semler asked. He felt it was because they wanted to look big and solid, but were dragging the staff two hours across town because of that. As a result they now have 14 different offices that people can work from, according to where they live or where their meetings are on a particular day.

Tech.

Chances are if you ever popped corn, it was in a microwave oven, which is one of the best "happy accident" stories ever. Percy Spencer, a self-taught American engineer, was working in a lab testing magnetrons, the high-powered vacuum tubes inside radars. He had a candy bar in his pocket, but later when he came to eat it, it had melted. What the ...? **"Why did my candy bar melt?"** he wondered. Which led him to backtrack and work out that the magnetron was actually emitting micro waves which heated and melted his food. Aha!

Engineers Carl Looney and Chuck Rockwell at Armstrong set about looking for cost-saving opportunities in their range of Armstrong Hunt unit heaters. Two questions proved powerful in uncovering unnecessary extra materials and functionality on 90% of units manufactured. **"Why do we do it this way? Why is this part needed?"** Now, cast a fresh eye on your products and ask these questions.

On a well-deserved beach holiday, the inventor Roy Land (who earned an amount of patents second only to Edison) was taking photos of his 3-year old daughter, Jennifer, on the beach one day. She was excited and wanted to see the pictures NOW! **"Why do we have to wait for the pictures, Daddy?"** The innocent child's question got Roy's brain racing, and resulted in the Polaroid instant photo system that could satisfy Jennifer by letting her see the images in less than 60 seconds. See how his line of questioning developed in the next step.

"Why aren't all enterprise software applications built like Amazon and eBay?" was the question that popped to the relaxed mind of Marc Benioff after swimming with dolphins off the coast of Hawaii. To date, software was still being delivered via CDs and downloaded manually by the user. Answering that question, Salesforce changed the software model to the downloadable model we know today.

Steve Jobs was a famous meditator, and enjoyed quietness. Which is why he probably noticed the whirring of a fan inside computers more than anyone else. **"Why does a computer need a fan?"** he asked. Thus pushed, engineers of later models of the Mac managed to disperse the heat in other ways , opening the door for ever-slimmer models.

Another super-challenge came from Samsung in the form of the question: **"Why isn't there a middle category of device, in between a laptop and a smartphone? What if we build one?"** Samsung thus introduced the phablet.

And that is a great example of how good Why questions often suggest and segue into great What If questions.

"After reading Why questions, I realized that a lot of Why questions can be reframed as What If," Kapil Kane, head of R&D at Intel China, tells me after reading this manuscript. "For example, "Why should I have to pay their late fees?" in the Netflix example above can be reframed to "What If I didn't have to pay the late fees?" Exactly! It propels forward momentum.

So What If we tackle those next?

WHAT IF? QUESTIONS

In February 2017 I was lucky enough to be sitting in the front row, ringside, for a masterclass (as part of Victoria Labalme's Rock the Room workshop) at the Los Angeles Theater Centre on storytelling by Pete Docter, the writer and director behind several of Pixar's biggest hits, including *Monster's Inc*, *Toy Story*, *Up*, etc.

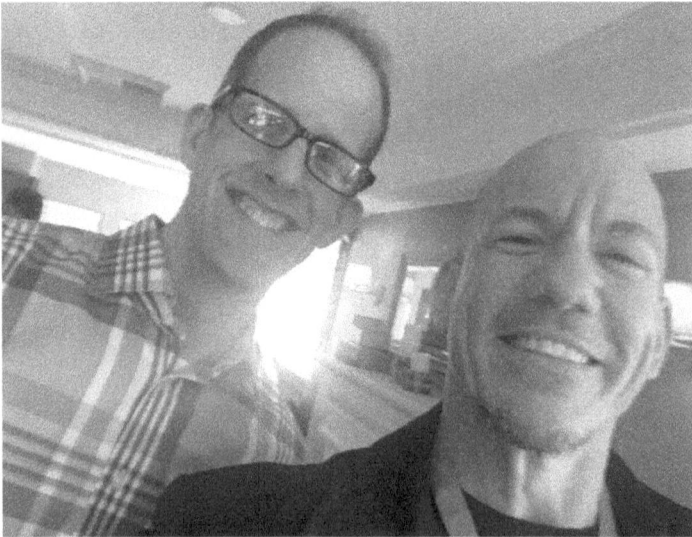

One of these goofballs has 8 Oscar nominations, the other none ... yet.

What a treat! An insight into how some of the most creative minds in business work, and especially the role of feelings and emotions in storytelling. So it got me thinking how Pixar use questions as part of the creative process. Turns out questions, especially What If questions, are absolutely the star of their show.

"At Pixar these What Ifs are not only fun but a simple way to kick off the whole creative process," says Valerie LaPointe, story artist. "What If questions invite the imagination into a story you want to explore."

"What Ifs really drive that imagination," agrees director, Mark Andrews, the man behind *The Incredibles* and *Brave*. His colleague, story artist Kristen Lester, adds: "The best What Ifs are like a key that unlock a door."

Ooh – I like it! So how do they work exactly? Animator and story artist, Sanjay Patel explains: "It really shuts down the logic part of your brain, and lets you engage the dream part of the brain, and somehow it opens the doors to your imagination."

This is the land of infinite possibility. That's why What If questions are my favourite.

We take our Why questions, that did the initial challenging, and catapult ourselves forward in Crazyville!

A creative leap into Lah Lah Land.

"So what happens if a werewolf bites a goldfish?" Neil Gaiman – Hugo Award-winning fiction writer – playfully posits as the type of creative leap a writer might make in searching for a storyline.

And Felicia Yap, Malaysian-born author of the thriller *Yesterday,* based her novel on the creative premise: **"What if you couldn't remember yesterday?"** The characters are divided between Monos (who have a one-day memory) and elite Duos (who can remember two). As a bonus, the subhead of her novel is a How question: **"How do you solve a murder when you only remember yesterday?"** She gained a six-figure deal as a first-time author on the back of this high concept approach.

All that old school stuff about suspending judgment etc still holds true. Because here you are throwing up new creative alternatives. Do not hold yourself back with the usual self-editing boring bullshit like no budget, tight deadlines, technology that hasn't been invented yet, and breaking the laws of physics.

(Actually, Elon Musk might just have something to say about that last one ...)

Everything is possible in the Kingdom of Creativity.

Only later in the process after brainstorming the solution will we be looking to "land" the idea and make it a practical reality.

So, for now, enjoy the hedonistic freedom ... of defying convention, defying gravity, and defying your boss and/or the industry leader.

TO CREATE KILLER WHAT IF? QUESTIONS I FAVOUR THESE 3 DISRUPTIVE TECHNIQUES:

- **REVERSING**
- **STRETCHING**
- **SQUEEZING**

BEEP, BEEP, BEEP, BEEP. REVERSING.

For example, let's go back to the Dyson hand dryer example. If the assumption is we *must* have a towel, the Why question becomes "Why must we have a towel?", then the reversal is **"What if we have NO towel?"**

You reversed it. You turned it upside down. You flipped it on its head.

And from this comes dangerous energy. The kind of dangerous energy that causes people to laugh or giggle in self-preservation.

Look no further than Dyson for another example of reversal. **"What if a fan has NO blade?"** Haha! All hail the AirBlade.

See what I mean?

It's the boldest, bravest, bestest way to turn the world upside down, and have a look at it from that angle.

Remember, we're not trying to solve the problem at this stage, we're trying to create a Killer Question that gives us a very different starting point for thinking and/or a better problem to solve.

Logical thinking gets us from A to B. Terrain that's clearly marked on the map, because everyone's been there before. Reverse-angle What If? questions drop us off in the middle of nowhere, without Google Maps, and we need to start from there and work out what we're doing there and why no one visited that place before. It's a different starting point for thinking. Gold dust.

To quote the sage David Byrne from Talking Heads' *Once In a Lifetime*: "And you may ask yourself, Well … how did I get here?" (Millennials, I'll give you a minute to Google it.)

It's not important *how* you got there, just the fact that you did.

S-T-R-E-T-C-H-I-N-G THE TRUTH.

Another great go-to technique with What If questions is to stretch your assumption.

So, to do that we make it bigger.

We can do this by multiplying your thing x 2. Or by

10. Or 100. Just keep adding zeroes to it.

Back to our fan example: **"What if we have 1000 blades?"**

To give you some recent examples. Doing some challenging in a workshop with GE Healthcare, we talked about one of the assumptions of MRI scans being that it was done one patient at a time.

Which led us to the What If stretch of **"What if we could scan 10 patients at a time?"** Haha! **"What if we could scan 100 patients at a time?"** Hahaha!

(In a later ideation round, the idea of a train-like carriage full of patients steaming into an open magnetic field was proposed.)

Or with DaimlerBenz's R&D guys we stretched the assumption of two headlights. What if it had 100. Or 1000?

It's not that silly in this age of LEDs – especially when we rid ourselves of the original dominant logic that we needed two headlights because horse-drawn carriages had two, one on each side of the horse. Well, guess what, hipsters? We don't have horses anymore so that original assumptive factoid can disappear.

SQUEEZING THE LIFE *INTO* IT.

This is all about making it smaller, less. Miniaturization. Think of it as a bonsai plant compared to your full sized flower.

So with squeezing, we take your Why question then vacuum-pack and shrink-wrap it.

So we divide it by 2. Or remove a zero or three. Then stand back and see what suggestive shape your question takes then.

"What if our car had 3 wheels? Two wheels? One wheel?"

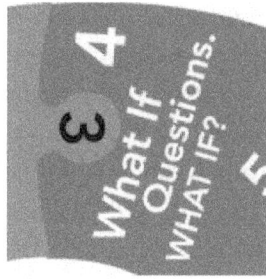

SOME KILLER WHAT IF? QUESTIONS.

Entertainment.

For *Toy Story*, the half-billion dollar question was **"What if our toys around us were actually sentient and can come alive?"** says Sanjay Patel. A deceptively simple question that changed the course of movie-making. And **"What if a rat wanted to cook haute cuisine?"** was the playful question that set *Ratatouille* in motion, according to Domee Shi, storyboard artist.

JK Rowling's $21 billion question, conceived as she sat on a train, returning from yet another dispiriting meeting with a publisher who rejected her work: **"What if a little boy embarked on a train that enabled him to escape the boring adult world and enter a place where he was powerful?"**

Ever wonder what kick-started the idea of KickStarter? Well, founder Perry Chen wanted to bring a band to a jazz fest he was organizing. But, it was going to be a big out-of-pocket undertaking with no known outcome of success. **"What if we could ask those who might enjoy jazzfest to commit to buying tickets?"** he thought. If the threshold was reached, it was on. If not, it went away. Thus the idea of pre-pledging was planted. He's now sitting on a buzzing crowd-funding business valued at around $400,000,000.

Walt Disney mused on a question that revolutionized entertainment in the form of theme parks. **"What if this amusement park could be like a movie bought to life?"** This set the groundwork for Disney delivering magic. Every team member from Mickey Mouse down to the janitor was a "cast member," charged with delivering that magic. Because everyone played a starring role in this movie.

Photography.

Recall Roy Land's young daughter's impatience at wondering why the photos were not immediately viewable. Roy's next question became **"What if you could somehow have a darkroom inside a camera?"** This was a lightbulb moment on how a Polaroid camera might be like a self-contained portable photo lab.

Hospitality.

"What if we provide more than just a mattress to sleep on?" pushed Joe Gebbia and flatmates riffing into the realms of not just offering an airbed and Coco Pops to visitors to their house, but to the possibility of what else this offering could become. **"What if we could create this same experience in every major city?"** A game-changing platform innovation, with AirBnB worth $31 billion, as it turned out.

And Joe also uses one of my favourite all-purpose sector-agnostic disruptive questions: **"What if we could start with a blank page?"** Meaning, if our corporate history and sunk costs (financial and emotional) were not weighing us down and skewing us towards certain ideas and practices and habits, what should we *really* be doing and how would we approach it differently? Would we still be making the same things the same way? Really???

This is a HUGE question which drives us away from legacy thinking. Please take a minute to think about that now.

And as AirBnB faces pushback from the legacy hospitality industry and nervous politicos in some quarters of the world, a great question arises: **"What if politicians used the sharing economy?"**asked David Leyonhjelm, himself an Australian senator. He posits that politicians, staffers and public servants should be encouraged to use shared-economy solutions in their work travel, to get to know the safety and efficiency of such services. Because he feels the shared economy is seen as a threat to governments, because it delivers all of its self-regulated benefits without red tape and intervention. As Ronald Reagan once said: "Government is not the solution to the problem – government *is* the problem."

Electrical appliances.

Bacon. Aah, everyone loves bacon, right? Even Sir Francis Bacon because he developed the refrigerator in which bacon is stored these days. **"What if you could preserve meat with ice? (It came into my lord's thoughts, why flesh might not be preserved, as in salt.)"** was the question that drove that discovery. A few centuries later, on the opposite side of the world in Alaska, that question was answered for Clarence Birdseye when he was taught to fish by the Inuit, who hauled in fish from under the ice cap in Newfoundland. He noticed that with temperatures on land a decidedly chilly – 40 degrees, the fish froze almost immediately. He also made the observation that the fish tasted far better than what he'd experienced even in good New York Restaurants.

"What if there were no bag? What if you could make an entirely bagless vacuum cleaner?"pondered (now Sir) James Dyson, after gleaning insights onto what sucked – or rather, what didn't suck — about the incumbent model of vacuums. This, combined with cross-pollinating his knowledge of centrifuges turned out to be the winning ticket.

Education.
"**What would happen if we turned the university inside out? What if we moved course content to the outside, as resources to be used?**" asks serial provocateur and former PARC director, John Seely Brown, from University of Southern California. Stay tuned!

Agriculture.
"**What if I took 1 square foot on the roof of the tallest building in New York City?**" posed aeroponic urban farm pioneer, Caleb Harper, from MIT. He's now reshaping how we think of urban spaces as potential "farmland" to feed an increasingly urbanized world.

Exploration.
Alan Eustace is by all accounts a mild-mannered guy who works as a SVP of Knowledge at Google. Many of his colleagues did not know the crazy shit he got up to at weekends, such as free-falling from the stratosphere. "**What if you could design a system that would allow humans to explore the stratosphere as easily and safely as they do they ocean?**" he wondered. This ended up being the design brief for the suit and system he was kitted out in during his successful attempt at the world's highest free-fall jump from 41km (that's right, not inches, centimetres or even metres, *kilometres*!) Cripes – that's a vertical marathon!

E-cigarettes.
The idea apparently came to him in his sleep, but manifested itself to Hon Lik in the form of the rather wordy

question: **"What if there was a way to deliver both a nicotine hit and something approximating the satisfaction of inhaling smoke, without the tar and noxious carcinogens?"** The answer was the e-cigarette which is carving a huge market share of the traditional tobacco market, and a massive share of the "I'm quitting smoking" market.

Electricity.

"What if we no longer needed electricity to produce light?" asked Sandra Rey, which led her down the track of biomimicry, and finally to creation of the Glowee lights using bioluminescent light, which is naturally created by marine animals such as jellyfish, algae squid, etc.

Tech.

Professor Timothy Leighton, and his colleagues at the University of Southampton, were musing on pulses and sonar. Suddenly he found himself doing some nifty perception shifting, asking: **"What pulse would I use if I were a dolphin?"** This line of investigation led him to invent the Twin Inverted Pulse Sonar (TWIPS), a new kind of underwater sonar device that can detect objects through bubble clouds that would effectively blind standard sonar.

"What if the user could type instructions into the computer that were easier to memorise than pure machine code?" asked Grace Hopper, an incredible woman who was not only a female Rear Admiral in the US Navy but also a computer scientist. She popularized the idea of machine-independent programming languages in the 60s, which led to the development of COBOL, an early high-level computer programming language still in wide use today.

These days that question might be updated to **"What if programming could be in languages such as Chinese,**

Spanish, Arabic, and not just English?" (More a sort of What If/Then scenario ...)

Still on languages of sorts, student Joseph Woodland once overheard a supermarket executive briefing his college Dean on developing a better way to track products and inventory. Woodland's Dean declined the challenge, but, intrigued, Woodland took it upon himself to pursue this creative challenge. A little later on holiday at the beach he was absent mindedly raking his fingers in the sand, making random patterns of wide and narrow lines. As a former Boy Scout he was aware of Morse code, and the patterns echoed it. **"What if Morse Code, with its elegant simplicity and limitless combinatorial potential, could be adapted graphically?"** became his Killer Question. The unique lined patterns, which became bar codes, could identify and track individual products.

Back in the Jurassic age of the internet, two crack code-breaking students at Stanford, William Diffie and Martin Hellman, were puzzled by the cryptology practices on the internet. Basically Party A and Party B both had to have the same padlock and same key if they were to be able to open, read and close each others' messages securely. **"What if both parties did not need to same key?"** they idly pondered. That question violently reversed the accepted logic of the day, and further investigation of an obscure mathematical practice of one-way functions, made them feel they were onto something. Indeed, later refinement and development on one-way cyphers by a team at MIT unlocked the explosive potential of e-commerce on the internet as we know it today.

So Jeff Bezos and Jack Ma have a lot to thank Diffie and Hellman for.

Struggling with motivation spurred Jia Jiang into thinking: **"What if I could develop an app that would issue some kind of point or credit for fulfilling a promise?"** While this didn't bear any fruit for him, motivational apps like Fabulous, Strides and Habit Bull deliver on his line of thinking.

Music.

Steve Jobs was notoriously passionate about music, with U2, the Grateful Dead and Bob Dylan among his high-rotational plays. Once MP3 technology came along, his question was **"What if we created an MP3 player that could hold 1000 songs and still fit in your pocket?"** This informed the thinking that led to the revolutionary iPod.

Tim Westergren was a music producer who also had a passion for biology and new technologies. After reading an article in a biology magazine, a thought popped to his mind: **"What if we could map the DNA of music?"** He started mapping out songs manually, tagging them by 450 genomes per song to enable rich search of suggestions of stuff you might like, not just by genre, but by vocal style, rhythm, instrumentation, etc.

This labour intensive work paid off, earning Pandora more than 80,000,000 active listeners and over $750m in annual revenues.

Consumer Goods.

The boffins at P&G were wrestling with a stubborn problem about stain removal from garments from kids mucking about, playing sports etc which then contaminated other garments in the wash. **"What if that soil never got to bond on the second garment to begin with?"** This lead to a further question: **"What if we could prevent the bonding** reaction in the washing machine?" The net result was a seismic shift in their search, from looking for chemicals that removed dirt to chemicals that prevented redepositing. The result? The most effective Tide detergent ever produced.

There was also a brainstorm session on oral hygiene for kids at P&G that led Paul Smith to ponder the following question: **"What if we could make brushing your teeth so much fun, kids actually want to do it?"** This in turn led to other What If creative stimuli questions, such as **"What if when you brushed your teeth, the toothpaste turned bright purple?"** and **"What if the tube lit up like a Christmas tree when you squeezed it?"** and **"What if we put a prize at the end of the tube like in a Cracker Jack box?"**

Media.

We've already seen how Reed Hastings asked why late fees were a thing, which segued to his provocative cross-pollinatory question of: **"What if a video rental business were run like a health club?"** It happened because he'd just come from his gym, which was run on a monthly subscription model, now familiar to streamers worldwide.

Office supplies.

"What if we could paint over our mistakes?" moved Betty Nesmith further along the thinking pipeline after observing decorators at her bank simply painting over their mistakes as they dressed the windows for Christmas. This led to the development of Tippex, white-out for typists.

Fashion.

"What if some company started selling socks that didn't match?" is a question that could come straight from busting the assumption that socks are always sold in pairs, and socks are always matching. "Life is too short for matching socks," claims the website of Solmate Socks.

When Margaret Wood, a native American designer of Navajo and Seminole descent, was growing up, she noticed that everyone only had one native formalwear item in their wardrobe. Which got her thinking: **"What if I could make something to wear to the office or everyday, not just on special formal occasions?"** She started Native American Fashions, and has since become an author and expert on the subject, with her artifacts even exhibited in museums.

Alarm Clocks.

Anyone who has ever pushed the "snooze" button, then pushed it again, will relate to this one. **"What if it was harder to turn off the alarm clock? What if your alarm clock forced you to get out of bed and chase after it?"** This led Gauri Nanda to the idea that an alarm clock could be fitted with wheels, and set in motion, jumping off the bedside table, when her alarm rang. After several rounds of hacking low-res mockups together, the vibrant Clocky became a reality, selling half a million units in its first year.

Suitcases.

Another insight from the power of observation and associative thinking, when a wheeled skid was seen being pushed through an airport with a heavy load on it, surrounded by passengers struggling with heavy luggage. **"What if I put wheels on these suitcases?"** was the insight from Bernard Sadow that led to the creation of a four-wheeled lay-flat suitcase, further fine-tuned by pilot Robert Plath, who thought two wheels and a long handle would be even better. Today, Rollaboard cases, and their imitators are seen and used everywhere.

Banking/ Finance.

The ever-curious Jack Dorsey, fresh in the throes of twitter mega-stardom, had been having drinks with an associate in a pub, when his friend mentioned that it was possible to read magnetic cards through the ear-phone jack (no relation) of a smart phone. How did someone find this out? At the same time an artist friend of his was bemoaning the fact that he couldn't take credit card payments without being a merchant, with all the red tape and hassle that went with that.

Which got Jack thinking: **"What if all you needed to swipe a credit card was a smart phone or tablet?"** The answer was fintech disruptor, Square, which has democratized the payments market with its plug-and-pay dongle.

"What if we could invest as a means, not as an end?" is the big question that drove Jacqueline Novogratz to found non-profit social entrepreneurship fund, Acumen. Its point of departure is that it combined the best of VC world with philanthropy, ploughing back profits into new ventures and start-ups.

Guitar strings.

We met Dave Evans from Gore back in the Why? section. The ending to Ride-On cables was an even happier one when Evans asked **"What if I put plastic coating on guitar strings?"** to get around the issue of a muffled sound with aging. So they applied the same technology to guitar strings, resulting in the Elixir range, which musicians are happy to pay 3 x the usual rate for because they sound better and last longer.

Company Culture.

Big brave ballsy questions are not just for product development. Google asks the question **"What if we could**

create the experience of a TED conference, every day within the company?" This gives it the free-flowing idea-sharing culture it prides itself on. They also stage lunchtime sessions, inviting everyone from rappers to beat-boxers to comedians, whatever, to edutain them.

e-Commerce.

Asking questions doesn't need to be an exercise in rocket science, in fact the power often comes from the basic broad insight rather than the semantics. So when Jeff Bezos was a young analyst pouring over data, he discovered that the fledgling thing called e-commerce had grown by over 2300% in the previous 12 months. But he noticed something that was not in the top 10 of items sold. **"What if I could use the internet to sell books at low price points?"**

You see, it's not really how the question is phrased, as much as that that simple question was asked at all. Result: Amazon, doing over $60 billion in revenues annually.

eBay's Pierre Omidyar has a Swiss Army knife question for all occasions: **"What if we did the opposite of this? What would happen then?"** Bam! Feel the explosive power of that.

Health.

Bill Gates is to be lauded for his single-minded determination to answer one question: **"What if we could rid the world of malaria?"** They are throwing millions if not billions at this, but I wonder if they have the right How question to solve this problem?

BONUS: SOME COOL EXTRA WHAT? QUESTIONS.

While What If questions are the cue to catch a bus to Crazyville in our thinking, What questions can play a powerful role too. So let's take a little detour from our template to contemplate some game-changing What questions ... all aboard!

"What would dramatically affect the future in a positive way?" is the general question Elon Musk sets for himself to shape and inform the challenges for Tesla, SpaceX and Solar City. Gee, that opens the skies up nice and wide for blue sky thinking, doesn't it?

His former partner in PayPal, Peter Thiel, also has a great provocative question: **"What is something you believe that almost no one agrees with you on?"** Having such a contrarian stance on something might be a long hard road to world seeing it your way, but this is the nature of most big game-changing ideas.

My answer to that question would be that I believe that countries should be able to outsource their government to other countries and authorities who are capable of managing it properly and better. Government is way too important to be left to the local incompetent politicos alone in most cases. Ooh, I know! That rankles doesn't it? Exactly!

Regina Dugan was director at Defense Advanced Research Projects Agency (DARPA) before moving across to Google. She kickstarted a movement with her TED talk in which she tells us the central question that guided her team's work at the agency was: **"What would you attempt to do if you knew you could not fail?"** Meaning, remove the safety nets, the fear of being booted out of your job, the blinkers from your mind, and think what's wildly possible? Some of the surprising answers that came out of that unfettered mindset at DARPA were a robotic hummingbird, a prosthetic arm controlled by thought, and, even, the internet as we know it.

AG Lafley, while helming P&G, drove himself personally with this quest(ion): **"What will I choose to be**

curious about on Monday morning?" This fed his lifelong learning stance, and instilled a curiosity into the organization.

Steve Jobs was the master of intuiting latent demand, with his much-famed disdain of consumer research groups. Rather than asking **"How do other stores do retail?"** he asked **"What do customers REALLY want, even though they might not yet realize it?"** Which brings to mind Henry Ford's famous utterance: "If I'd asked people what they wanted, they would have said faster horses."

So always make sure you are solving real customer problems by observing and feeling pain points and peeves, not asking.

Which is why Nilesh Pattayanak, MD of Bombardier for South Asia, says: "We are in the business of *time*." That's what his high-flying customers actually want and need – more time to get shit done. Fast jets are just one way to achieve that.

This next one I often use in workshops to stretch people's possibility thinking. It comes from Aaron Levie, the founder of Box (like DropBox but they dropped the Drop part). **"What would blow our customers' minds?"** As his personal net worth has long-since exploded through the $100,000,000 mark, I guess he knows …

Why not take some time to riff on that now … and really push yourself to a point just on the other side of extreme.

Another guy who imparts tremendous flipping (literally!) energy with his questioning is Jay Z (that's Mr Beyonce to you). When he consults with youth brands, he's known to bandy around these What? questions:

"What would it look like to break this?" Yeah! Feel the creative destruction!

"What would it look like to do everything 'perfectly wrong'?" This one always elicits titters of nervous laughter in workshops from people who've been toe-ing the party line groupthink in their big companies, with doing things repeatedly right drummed into them (if not actually tattooed on their foreheads).

Then finally his third disruptive question is: **"What does it look like to flip that on its head?"**

Turning things upside down and looking from a different angle always elicits dramatic new angles and approaches.

I hope you enjoyed that exploratory side track.

So, let's move on to How? questions, which set us the challenge to be solved, or the opportunity to be explored.

HOW? QUESTIONS

I've always been a dog person, rather than a cat person. But last year when my new partner, Mam, moved in, she came along with two kittens.

They were cute enough, Maji being a grey Persian, and her brother Samlee being white (his name means 'cotton' in Thai).

But what made me really warm to them was their contagious curiosity. I couldn't move a newspaper, rustle a packet, flick a pencil, or do anything without them at least cocking a head, or sneaking up in ninja-like fashion, to get to the bottom of what was going on. They *had* to know. And so far, contrary to the proverb, it hasn't killed them yet.

Creative types are driven by curiosity. We want to know what's behind the thing that we see. What's causing that?

"When we want to know something but don't," Chip and Dan Heath tell us in *Make it Stick*. "It's like having an itch we need to scratch. To take away the pain we need to fill the knowledge gap."

When we feel the gap, we want, no, *need* to fill it. Because humans love closure, and the search for it is part of our brain's quest for efficiency.

When Chip Conley was brought on board at AirBNB, he felt a little out of water. Because he'd come from the "old school" of boutique hoteliers, and was a good couple of decades older than most of his geeky colleagues.

"I learned that my best tactic was to reconceive my bewilderment as curiosity," he says, "and give free rein to it. I asked a lot of Why questions and What If questions, forsaking the What and How questions on which most senior leaders focus."

Turns out he did the right thing ...

Master of persuasion, Dr Robert Cialdini's research shows that as we become psychologically closer to a certain matter or setting, we become more focused on "how" issues than "why" issues.

Which makes perfect sense in the flow of our Innovation Question Formulation System.

"As a general rule, asking 'why' yields more abstract statements and asking 'how' yields specific statements," according to Stanford d.School's method card on Why-How Laddering. "Often times abstract statements are more meaningful but not as directly actionable, and the opposite is true of more specific statements."

By the time we get to How questions, the process is far more convergent. We are looking now to land it. Bring all that craziness to reality. Make it happen.

Avoid pre-loading your question with a hinted solution to lead the jury, or shape the question to point your question to a preferred answer. It will close down the creative options available.

For example, your question shouldn't be **"How might we reduce absenteeism by offering workers money for each sick leave day they don't take?"** This exercise would be better served by a broader exploratory approach such as **"How might we reward our team for not taking sick leave?"** or **"How might we reward our team for staying healthy?"** which might even lead to **"How might we keep our team healthier?"**

SO *HOW?*

Jonas Salk and Einstein instinctively knew what neuroscience now tells us: Questions create a knowledge gap that the brain fights to close. Some call it a "Curiosity Gap."

"Curiosity happens when we feel a gap in our knowledge," notes George Loewenstein, from Carnegie Mellon University, who pioneered the information gap theory of curiosity.

Explaining this in WIRED magazine, Jonah Lehrer elaborates that curiosity tends to follow an inverted **U** shaped curve: "So that we're most curious when we know a little about a subject (our curiosity has been piqued) but not too much (we're still uncertain about the answer)."

The venerable former research director at PARC Xerox and other Silicon Valley ventures, John Seely Brown, goes as far as saying, "Curiosity is a new agent of learning," because of its very nature of making us lean forward towards something new or different or tantalising.

Lehrer calls it a "mosquito bite on the brain." It's the gap between what we know and what we want to know. But can we choose which mosquito infects us? Turns out, yes ...

"A completed task is a closed loop," says Amy Herman in *Visual Intelligence*. "An incomplete task is an open loop that uses up cognitive energy searching for a solution or worrying there isn't one yet."

The Curiosity Gap is famously used as the "cliff hanger" technique by TV series writers who will finish the action at a certain point, making sure we must tune in next week to see if the guy gets the girl, or if the bad guy comes back to life, etc. Or in TV game shows: **"And the answer ... will be revealed after this break. Don't go away!"** Aaargh!

It's also the go-to technique for masters of click bait headlines, such as:

"This elephant just got kicked in the balls by a kid. See what happens next."

This recent example from the *Sydney Morning Herald* created the cognitive gap well ...

"I wish I hadn't gone to work that day. What artist saw would rock the art world."

One of my favourite blogs, *PsyBlog*, uses curiosity gaps all the time – I'm sure their click-through rates are among the highest in the business (mind you, if *they* don't know how to manipulate us, who would?). Some examples just from the past week or so at time of writing ...

"The Eye Movements That Signal Someone Is Into You."

"This Fruit Reverses Brain Ageing."

"The Type Of Food That Destroys Cognitive Function."

"How do you spark curiosity?" asks Chris Anderson, in his book *TED Talks*. "The obvious way is to ask a question. But not just any question. A surprise question."

So, Curiosity Gap questions are a very deliberate way for us to set wonderful challenges for our super-computing subconscious. After all, it's way more powerful than our conscious mind, with millions times more bandwidth and crunch-power.

"Are you working too hard? Here's why."

"Six types of investor – do you know which group you're in?"

So the most productive format becomes:

"HERE'S SOMETHING YOU KNOW. NOW HERE'S WHAT YOU'RE MISSING."

For example:

"You know sleep is good for you. But how much sleep is bad for you?"

They tease and don't disclose the full answer, yet promise what you now presumably want to know.

SETTING CHALLENGES TO BRAINSTORM (CONSCIOUSLY OR SUB-CONSCIOUSLY)

Perhaps the best tip I can give you here is to put questions in the form of:

"HOW MIGHT WE ...?"

This format is the work of former P&G exec, Min Basadur, who championed its use due to the fact that the word "might" still leaves the solution creatively open to possibility (compared to the more proscriptive "could" or "should"). Also, the use of the royal "we" speaks to collaboration, teamwork, open-sourcing or even crowd-sourcing solutions. It moves us away from the lone wolf creative genius paradigm.

Thanks to some early adopters of this format in Silicon Valley, and their moving from company to company, it's now well entrenched in the usual suspect companies such as IDEO, Facebook, Google, etc.

"Great What if and How Might We questions leave us hanging and the subconscious will not rest until it is solved," confirm the Heath brothers.

So, seed your mind with killer How Might We questions. Then walk away from it.

This works because one of the most solid and consistent findings in all of creativity research is that there is no creativity without slack time. We must withdraw physically or mentally from the problem in order to solve it best.

This can be by playing on Facebook or Twitter for 10 minutes. Or taking a 15 minute power nap. Sleeping on it overnight. Or, the granddaddy of them all, by flying from New York to the Caribbean like Citibank's John Reed did, swanning around the pool bar of a resort, and generating a 20-page "Memo from the Beach" in which he outlined a profitable model for credit cards (that's right, banks didn't know how to do that in the early 70s) and envisioned the full-featured all-singing all-dancing ATM operated by a plastic card.

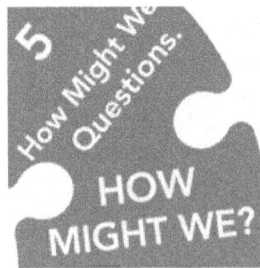

SOME KILLER HOW QUESTIONS

So let's get down to the business end of the tournament, at look at some How questions that were the springboard for some mind-blowingly explosive thinking.

Jailing jihadists.

Literally, a killer question in this case: **"How can you jail extremists without creating more terrorists?"** pose journalists Nino Bucci and Rachel Olding in looking at whether it's best to take an isolationist hard-line approach to their internment, or better to have an inclusive program of dispersal. The jury is still out as the world grapples with this new issue.

Communications & Media.

Back in the 60s, psychologist Stanley Milgram was trying to better understand the "small world" problem. Are we all in a parallel universe, or are we actually closer connected than we ever imagined? His springboard question was: **"How does an idea or a trend or a piece of news travel through a population?"** By investigating this, experimenting with selecting 160 random people from Nebraska and asking them to get a package to a certain stockbroker in Boston via someone they knew. This gave rise to what we popularly know today as the "Six Degrees of Separation" rule.

One field that has been digitally disrupted more noticeably than others is the print media. As a result, there are a slew of people trying to tackle this to make their publication, blog, vlog, and other analog and/or digital content, pop.

Skateboarder turned and storyteller, Rob Dyrdek, keeps busy on many fronts with media, including the MTV program, *Ridiculousness*. Catering to the fickle channel-switching millennial viewer, Rob realizes he needs to make great or else. So there are two questions that guide him and his production crew: **"How can we relentlessly manufacture amazing?"** is the first one. That's a goodie – applicable to you, and every other business on the planet.

Take a minute to answer that question in your own context now. You're welcome!

The second question he asks of himself is **"How can I tell a story that's irresistibly shareable?"** If he can't, or the answer is he doesn't, his on-air career would be measured in nano-seconds in the modern social media environment.

A similar theme occupies the minds of Chip and Dan Heath, saying the question to ask is: **"How do we make people care about our messages?"** Their suggested solution is to use a piggybacking strategy in which ideas associate themselves with existing emotions, to create more care factor.

Former Saatchi's CEO, Kevin Roberts, was similarly consumed about having customers care rather than just interrupted. "The big question for me," he says, "has always been, **How do you get intimate with consumers without being invasive or insincere?"** This is a big challenge for marketeers trying to reach millennials in particular, but just about all age groups now resent interruption-style ads and marketing campaigns.

"How can you create a newsletter people will actually want to open?" is the challenge Cayleigh Parrish of *Fast Company* sets for herself to ensure readership and open rates remain engagingly high. She must be doing OK, because I opened that one.

And over at the venerable Gallup organization, their central question is: **"What do people want to read, and how do you give it them?"** Simple? Yup. But if you answer that, and deliver on it, that's all there is to know.

You could delete the word 'read' and substitute your own industry verb in there and see what happens. Try it now.

For example, for gamers: **"What do millennials want to *play*, and how do we give it to them?"**Or for automotive: **"What do people want to *drive*, and how do we give it to them?"**

Derek Thompson's book *Hit Makers* is well worth the read to understand why some ideas catch fire and others don't. Here's how he tackles the question of media in the New Economy: **"How do people want to experience news, entertainment and storytelling, whether the medium is word, images, or sounds?"**

Even IDEO has been weighing in on this, with partner Suzanne Gibbs Howard believing that collaboration between human storytellers and machines is more likely in the near future. **"How might the world's storytellers leverage knowledge and insights via AI to make their stories even more powerful, faster? Might AI be a prototyping tool?"**

Food.

Jeffrey Dunn had spent 20 years marketing Coca Cola, before he joined Bolthouse Farms. **"How do you make carrots cool?"** became his question, leading to cheeky kick-ass marketing slogans like "Eat 'em like junk food" which boosted sales of their baby carrots by 13%.

Visiting the scene of the Japanese tsunami in 2011 (which I also did) spurred some thought processes in Caleb Harper because the waste of farmland, the loss of hope, and the future of food security and farming really hit home: His family is in the grocery business and also raises crops and livestock in Southern USA. Together with his experience as an architect and engineer he designed hospitals and data centers. "It got me thinking: **How can I put my different skill sets together to make a difference?"** He realized that what was really needed is a data center for food, one that is not exposed to the natural environment. Which led him to aeroponics and the establishment of the City Farm Project.

"How can this be the next biggest concept out there in my category?" wondered Natasha Haus, co-founder of CoolHaus Ice Cream. A great example of unlimited stretch thinking, and letting off the hand brake on how your business is "supposed" to be. Their one food truck with architecturally influenced ice cream shapes and names created buzz at the first music festival they rocked up to, and now they are rocking sales of $7 million annually, with a national fleet of 10 mobile ice cream trucks and carts in LA, Dallas and NYC, plus you can find them in the freezer of your local Safeway, too.

"How do you Connect users to the Harvest in a world where attention spans are too short and divided to even keep a seedling alive?" That was the question Naked Juice asked OMD to launch their new product, Tomato Kick. It resulted in a super-cool social-media driven interactive PowerGarden in downtown Chicago, which picked up a Shorty Award for use of technology in the Food and Beverage sector.

Automotive.

"How do we not go back to where we were?" was Henry's grandson, Bill Ford's, way to avoid the complacency and fatness that he had seen Ford mired in, on the brink of bankruptcy before Allan Mulally took the helm. **"How do we stay lean and hungry? And how do we continue to foster innovation?"** completed his trinity of questions. Might these sector neutral questions be directly adaptable to *your* situation?

Mulally, for his part, came on board and told everyone that they'd been going broke for the past 40 years as a car company. **"How can we be the best mobility company?"** is the question he felt they should be answering. That ushered in a $20 billion positive turnaround in Ford's fortunes over the next 8 years.

The noun here is all-important. The key is your Strategic Aperture, your field of fire. Ask yourself: **"What business are we REALLY in?"** Macdonald's might ask itself: **"How can we** be the best show business company?" It's a very different question to answer than **"How can we be the best burger company?"**

"How can we create the most thermally efficient engine in the world?" is literally the driving question behind Andy Cowell and the Mercedes F1 team. This keeps their champions like Lewis Hamilton and Valtteri Bottas on the podium more often than not. A good example of a really specific technical question, which could easily have been the more generic **"How might we create the fastest engine in the world?"** which might not produce the engineering result needed.

Banking/ Finance.

"How to make Citibank's Treasury team in Asia routinely innovative?" is the mission question ASPAC COO Ani Filipova minted in a recent meeting with me, implying they want innovative thinking to be hard-baked into the DNA of everything they do.

Arkadi Kuhlmann was convinced that in the wake of White House bailouts and ongoing underperformance, the banking industry itself was bust. A broken model. So in 2000 he set about kickstarting a different idea, a different model that would stand its customers and itself in better stead over time.

These three questions were central to his thinking:
"How can we do something radically different?"
"How do we re-create and re-energize an industry?"
"How can we build a company around a big idea?"

That turbo-charging trio makes me salivate with anticipation.

The result was a brave new strategy for ING Direct USA, an internet-based savings bank, light on all the usual things a bank takes for granted, so instead it could deliver efficiencies in the area of low overhead cost, simplicity and speed.

By 2012 the out-performing business had become the benchmark performer in direct banking, and was sold to Capital One for US$9 billion.

Linda Rottenberg is acknowledged now as as one of Time's 100 "Innovators for the 21st Century." But it took a chat with an Argentinian taxi driver to spark a breakthrough insight in her. **"How can I possibly start my own company when I don't even have a garage?"** the driver, who happened to have a PhD in Physics, asked her. What resulted from that was the establishment of Endeavor, the world's leading high-impact entrepreneurship movement, which to date claims to have created 650,000 jobs through businesses it has spawned.

In 2016, Santa Fe Institute, known for its multi-sectoral cross-pollination, posed a provocative question: **"How might biology inform our efforts to manage financial markets?"** Wow! What an explosive showstopper! They then sponsored a meeting in Washington, DC, attended by eminent economists, ecologists, and evolutionary biologists who all answered the question from their angles to understand market behavior differently and better.

This could apply to YOUR business too.

Simply fill in the blanks below to stretch your mind into whole new shapes.

"HOW MIGHT [UNRELATED FIELD] INFORM OUR EFFORTS TO [DO OUR JOB]?"

Imagine if the world's leading accounting firm said: **"How might Cirque du Soleil inform our efforts**

to advise client companies?" Penny to a Pound you'd have some very fresh insights, approaches and perceptual breakthroughs.

In fact, I created that hypothetical example before coming across publicity for the C2 Conference, of which Cirque du Soleil is a founder. It emphasizes transformative "cross-industry" tracks of commerce and creativity, and, according to its blurb, the conference sets out to "forge new answers to this fundamental question: **How can business and thought leaders identify and seize the opportunities ahead?"** Its solution is a 2-day program in which leadership, technology, impact, art and design, plus marketing and media are tackled.

I like to see that organizations are beginning to concretely think in questions, and think more in terms of mission questions to relentlessly answer, rather than platitudinous mission statements to try and live up to.

Society.

In 2011 I had the pleasure of meeting Jon Jandai, a humble chap from the north-eastern Isaan region of Thailand. I was speaker coach for a TEDx on Creativity and Collaboration, and Jon was one of the speakers. One of the best things I did was get out of the way and allow him to tell his story in his utterly authentic and naturally humorous style. His anti-materialistic talk centred around the powerful question: **"How can we make life more easy?"** He nailed it and has racked up over 4.5 million views to date.

"How can we reduce loneliness in the digital world?" asks Dr Michelle Lim, psychologist at Swinburne University in Australia. Tinder would be my best guess!

And exploring a slightly more extreme social theme, that of springboarding from adversity, author Michaela Haas set herself a question to explore: **"How do some people survive changes, even great hardships, and seem to come out more determined, stronger, and wiser?"** The answer is the book *Bouncing Forward: Transforming Bad Breaks into Breakthroughs*.

Gerry Spence is one of the world's most well-known activist lawyers, having had the longest winning streak of any lawyer in the world ever (the last case he lost was in 1969!) But when he was just a young guy trying to find his place in the world, he had a question hovering in his head: **"How could a nobody ever become a somebody?"** That became his true north as he pulled himself up through the world.

The Bill and Melinda Gates Foundation and the poverty-tackling non-profit Acumen approached IDEO on the subject of safe drinking water. After swirling that around for a while, Tim Brown and team came up with this problem definition: **"How might we improve access to safe drinking water for the world's poorest people, and at the same time stimulate innovation amongst local water providers?"** A two-pronged approach which might seem a bit wordy. With that question in mind, they approached US designers and couple them with organisations on the ground in India and East Africa to tackle the problem to get a real design thinking approach going. Watch Tim's TED talk on this called 'Designers – Think Big!'

Dave Gilboa, co-founder of Warby Parker, is keen on asking: **"What can I do to make someone's life better?"** That's sure to lead him down many a further fertile and fulfilling path. Stay tuned! Or, better still, why don't *you* answer that question today and change the world?

e-Commerce.

"How can we dramatically bring down the price of glasses?" led Gilboa and his co-founders to see online as the way to sell glasses for a lot less. Of course there was resistance from the usual quarters, such as No-one's going to buy glasses online, etc. With Warby Parker's valuation over $1.2 billion currently, he clearly saw things differently.

Gwyneth Paltrow had a guiding question in mind to answer when she came to setting up her "modern lifestyle brand" website, Goop. **"How do I get through life in the best possible way?"** sets the direction for what products, services and solutions to include, and can also be the way her readers and consumers might view what the site does for them, too.

On a slightly larger scale, Jack Ma, of Alibaba set the broad goal of **"How can we help small businesses find global markets?"** for his world-beating e-commerce platform.

And Sean Parker, former president at Facebook, recently revealed the question that guided the thought process in those distant days when FB was just getting started: **"How do we consume as much of your time and conscious attention as possible?"** Well, they nailed that one!

Art.

One of the most amazing artists plying their trade this century is Malaysian, Red Hong Yi. Never heard of her? Get on board this visionary artist. Turns out that her question is: **"As an artist, how can I say goodbye to paintbrushes?"**

Well, check out her videos and see what she can create with coffee cups, basket balls, clothes pegs and celebrities like Yao Ming, Ai Wei Wei, Jackie Chan, etc. Suffice to say she absolutely crushes that question.

Music.

"How can I express myself through this score?" is what Norwegian violin virtuoso, composer and improviser

Henning Kraggerud, always asks when he sits down to play a piece. "I like to find an angle that is relevant to me today," he says.

Sport.
"How do you really develop the art of leadership? How can you be one of the great Wallaby captains?" is the question Australia's rugby coach Michael Cheika set to 25 year-old up-and-comer Michael Hooper, who took the reins of the team from retiring long-term skipper, Stephen Moore in 2017.

And Stateside, the Positive Coaching Alliance set itself the challenge: **"How do you clean up the bad behavior often associated with youth sports?"**

Delivery Drones.
Keller Rinaudo is working in some of the most inhospitable conditions in the world, as co-founder of Zip Line, delivering medicines to remote villages in Rwanda, Africa. **"How can we ensure that our Zip drones arrive safely at its destination, using more affordable components, at a smaller scale so it can service cases where lives are at risk?"** is the question they try and answer on a daily basis. Unwieldy, sure. But the stakes are high. And so are the speeds, at up to 70 mph. Given the precious payloads, the redundancy systems in place rival the scale of commercial airliners, with backup engines and computers in place.

Architecture.
Evgueni Filipov had a childhood obsession with origami, which has followed him into adulthood. His advisor, Professor Paulino has inspired him to pursue origami as a research direction for his PhD. "We are constantly trying to make

improvements and make origami architecture/engineering a reality," he tells me. So one of the big questions we are now pursuing is: **"How can we go beyond paper and use practical materials (such as woods, plastics, metals) with thickness to create large-scale origami?"**

"How do we humanize this mega-space?" is the question that's been guiding Moshie Safdie and his team as they create the latest terminal at Singapore's award winning Changi Airport. Looking more like a tropical playground, it includes the Forest Valley, Singapore's largest indoor garden, and the Rain Vortex, a 40m-tall indoor waterfall featuring a light and sound show at night.

Neuroscience and architecture are finding themselves to be odd but effective bedfellows. **"How do you build a space that optimizes learning in young children?"** is one question that Prof Thomas Albright, a vision scientist at the Salk Institute, is wrestling with.

AirBnB co-founder Joe Gebbia is a restless innovator and challenger, and is spending time re-connecting with his roots on the design side. Working with Japanese architect, Go Hasegawa, on the Cedar House project in the wilderness of Nara, Joe's brief was: **"How can architecture facilitate a deeper connection between guest and host?"** The prototyped answer seems to be the fusion of a private home with a communal village hall, and a Medici-effect mixture of local artisans working out of the space too.

Medicine.

Albright is also looking for solutions in the way hospitals are designed. **"How do you build a hospital that optimizes healing?"** he wonders. Surely not with the cold grey square blocks that most hospitals today are.

"**How can we get more incubators to the places that need them?**" was the final unlocking question for Jane Chen to develop Embrace portable incubators, that resemble a sleeping bag more than anything else, and use phase-shifting wax-like material to keep the baby's body warm for 4-6 hours from a simple soaking in boiling water for 5 minutes. No more heavy machinery, no more electricity, no more maintenance, no more high price tags.

English comedian Russell Howard was interviewing Richard Branson about the state of the National Health System in Britain and how it could be improved. Branson's answer was typically insightful, and in the form a How question: "**How can we put doctor and nurses back in control, instead of having this big wad of middle managers?**"

US Air Force doctor, Major Charles Chestnut, found himself on the frontlines during the Las Vegas concert shoot-up recently, called in to deal with the hundreds of innocents wounded by military-grade weapons. He and his team had just received training in "Austere Surgical Teams" – a kind of agile operating theatre in the field. As they set about treating the patients the question came to his mind: "**How would I treat these patients working in the middle of the desert with five-man teams?**" In the hectic nine-hour shift that followed, he'd worked his way through 40 sterile gowns, and given his teams a useful, but unwelcome, real life drill in their spartan new modus operandi.

Workplace.

The irrepressible Prof Albright is challenging this space (literally) too. "**How do you build a work environment that optimizes efficiency?**" is his question here. He believes neuroscience will provide many of the answers.

With the rise of the gig economy, and the need for flexible co-working spaces, Penelope Cottrill got thinking: **"How do you mesh the physical workplace with the rise of the team?"** The answer to her was Nous House co-work space, which provides fluidity and porousness for the gig economy.

Ricardo Semler at Semco Partners in Brazil likes to question how they recruit, by asking: **"How do we find people?"** He feels if they rethink the whole recruitment dance, they'll end up with longer, more fruitful and meaningful "marriages" with employees. His next question is: **"How can we take care of people?"** And their answer is NOT more HR. (When their headcount was 5,000 they only had 2 in HR.)

A restless thinker, he then started asking: **"How do you set up, design and organize for more wisdom?"** as opposed to just being in the Information Economy. Which led them to set up a school foundation, and ask a new question: **"How do you redesign school for wisdom?"** The result was Lumiar, where "disciplines are applied in a mosaic form of interdisciplinary knowledge" according to their website, and students can customize their curriculum according to their interests and competencies, with the aim of being exposed to 600 tiles of the mosaic by the time they are 17.

In the thought-provoking and compelling book, *Firms of Endearment*, the authors ask a question: **"How can a company be less self-focused, yet more successful?"** They posit that the most successful companies are run by CEOs who embrace more inclusive "both/and" thinking compared to limited and limiting either/or and if/then modes.

Another great question, well answered, is that of WL Gore. In trying to create a different corporate culture, which is more nimble, agile and less hierarchical, the question was: **"How do you make a company that's more like a car pool?"** Gore, one of the most consistently innovative companies for decades, has a fluid culture centred around self-forming teams.

When Australian actress Margot Robbie first moved to Hollywood, she was invisible and found the hardest thing was not knowing and connecting with the right powerful people. So she asked the question: **"How can I meet with the most established people?"** Her networking took a turn for the better from that angle, and we now know her as an Oscar-nominated actor and producer (*Wolf on Wall Street, I Tonya,* and others on her reel). She's now paying it forward for other up and coming film-makers and actors to help them to be seen and avoid the same problems as she had.

Tech.

In his best-selling book *Zero to One*, Peter Thiel riffs on how technology could be applied better to issues of humanity. **"How can computers help humans solve hard problems?"** This is a big fat hairy open-ended opportunity creation question, that many readers could take the ball and run with. Over to you.

When Jeff Bezos was puzzling over the next tech gizmo he could possibly create, he mulled a question: **"How do we get an intelligent personal assistant into the home of every Amazon customer?"** By zeroing in on this, he and his team were led towards what we now know as the Echo. "The Echo may be the closest thing we have to a Star trek computer at home," enthused CNET. And yes, it's the #1 seller on Amazon home speakers, not surprisingly.

Manufacturing.

Patagonia has long been admired for its sustainability stance. Its famous Black Friday ad was emailed to all its customers saying "Don't buy this jacket!" then outlining it preferred that its customers used its repair service rather than buying a new item. An ongoing question in the minds of management is **"How can we minimize environmental impact given that there is a tremendous carbon footprint operating a $570 million business?"** One way they've answered this is by buying up acres and acres of virgin land in Patagonia to protect it from development.

AG Lafley helmed P&G and saw them triple their innovation successes over his 12-year watch. In that time they also moved from 10 $1 billion brands to 24 and doubled their sales. No easy feat to turbo-charge a large company which was already kicking along well, into such extraordinary productivity. Of course there were many success factors, but Mr Lafley always had one question he wanted his teams to address: **"How can we give consumers their Saturday mornings back?"** The focus was on products that can get the housewife the hell out of the house so she can get on with real life and her weekend.

You could easily adapt that to fit the benefits and target moments of your product or solution, ie **"How can we give drivers their brain-dead commuting time back?"** or **"How can we give chemotherapy patients three more months of enjoyable quality end-of-life time?"**

Education.

Paul Taylor, a school principal in rural Australia is a passionate educator. So he founded and runs a teacher training conference called iOnTheFuture. **"How are we enabling our kids to be the best person, the best**

human, they can be?" is his guiding question to point our children's education in directions that helps them respond more successfully to the world around them, and ward off obsolescence by AI.

Chip and Dan Heath, the progressive thinking siblings, turned to education in their book, *Made to Stick*, and riffed on the idea of improving the tertiary education journey and destination. **"How do you turn a freshman into an architect?"** is their energetic question, the answer to which may well differ from traditional journey a university takes, if and when appropriately answered.

Airlines.

Here's that disruptive airline man Michael O'Leary again. **"The other airlines are asking how they can put up fares. We are asking how we could get rid of them?"** That seminal flip in a 2001 *Sunday Times* interview ushered in the lucrative era of add-on ancillary revenues in the low-cost sector.

Beauty.

The data was in. And it showed that only 2% of women thought that beauty advertising actually spoke to them. **"How can we talk to the other 98% of women about Dove products in a way that would resonate?"** asked Jess Weiner, advocate-consultant. The result was the creation of the Campaign for Real Beauty, using real women of all shapes, sizes and colours in their advertising, now rolling out to – and resonating in – markets worldwide.

Payments and Cars and Space Travel and Damn Near Everything else (given time) …

Elon Musk is a serial disruptor. So it may be surprising to hear him say, "I don't actually like to disrupt … that sounds disruptive! I am much more inclined to say, **"How can we make things better?"**

Those six deceptively simple yet powerful words can set in motion the willingness to explore new alternatives, which is the very starting point of creativity for ongoing *kaizen*-style improvement.

And let's finish with one that's applicable to EVERYONE's business …

"How in the world are we going to get an unfair advantage over our competitors?" asks Min-Liang Tan, CEO of Razer, the world leader in high-performance gaming hardware, software and systems. Basically their deal is everything for gamers, by gamers. And they seem to be winning extended plays judging by the fact that the Singaporean founder's personal net worth soared to $1.6 billion post their IPO in late 2017.

HARVESTING & PRIORITIZING YOUR QUESTIONS

Andso now you've got flipcharts full of questions. Insightful questions! Boring questions! Goofy questions! Completely off the wall questions that made the team laugh!

So which one is your explosive Killer Question?

How do we choose? Are there selection methods that work better than others? Gladly, yes.

"What we plant in the soil of contemplation, we shall reap in the harvest of action," a wise man (clearly not me) once said.

So now, Weary Question Farmers, we set down one set of tools, and pick up another.

My advice is that if time and space allow, come back another day, having left time for the dust to settle, and for perhaps some further subconscious percolation and incubation to have taken place.

Set the flipcharts (or your template worksheets) up in another room, an environment more suitable for convergent thinking. Because now you want to zero in on culling the best of what's been proposed. In a more logical, rational frame of mind.

The research points to collaborative selection techniques working better than, say, the boss going off on his own and choosing one winner.

To this end, I outline a few techniques for harvesting your Killer Questions.

RED DOTS.

Everyone gets 3 red sticky dots (you know the ones, little round circular things, sticky on one side). Each person gets to vote with 3 dots – which can be all placed against one answer, one dot against three different answers, or two on one and one on another. You get the idea.

Another tip. If there are senior people and others with greater influence in the room, they should go last, otherwise they will cause a herding and clustering around their choices.

Before voting commences, the facilitator should read out once again the initial objective of the Thinking Focus so as to re-calibrate our thinking and remind ourselves what we are really trying to do here.

Simply, the questions with the most dots are prioritized as the winners. Democracy in action.

But …

Selection criteria are important.

TYPICALLY, YOU MIGHT WANT TO CONSIDER THESE SELECTION CRITERIA:

1/ WHICH IS THE MOST URGENT PROBLEM TO SOLVE?

2/ WHICH IS THE MOST IMPORTANT PROBLEM TO SOLVE?

3/ WHICH IS THE MOST INTERESTING PROBLEM TO SOLVE?

You can see straightaway that each of these will yield very different results. So be clear on what criteria people are voting on.

Stanford d.School Selection methodology gives us some other criteria to consider. While in their case they intend it for ideas, I think it can apply equally effectively to questions too:

1/ The Rational choice
2/ The Most Likely to Delight
3/ The Darling of the Group
4/ The Long Shot.

Then get to it. Prioritize the three top scoring questions without fear nor favour ...

PERFECTING YOUR QUESTIONS

Once you've got your shortlisted winner or winners, that's not the end of it. There's still a lot more tweaking to be done to ensure it's the definitive Killer Question worth throwing time, money, and brainpower behind to solve.

This next step is about taking your Killer Question, or the top 3 prioritized ones, and giving them the TLC (Tender Loving Care) needed to make them really spark up the place. A Killer Question should make you want to reach for a welder's mask because you can't stand to stare at the brazen naked light it radiates.

KILLER QUESTION BASIC FORMULA.

Whenever facilitating question storming or ideation workshops, I usually insist on questions being output in this format:

"HOW MIGHT WE (ACHIEVE OUR OBJECTIVE)?

Improving and Perfecting Killer Questions.

Your question might be too broad. Too narrow. Too high. Too low. Too active. Too passive ... too ... not compelling enough. It must make you lose sleep for impatiently wanting to solve it.

Open-ended or Closed-ended.

If the question leads you to a yes-no, black-white, binary option answer, it means it's closed-ended. **"Can we motivate our teams with money?"** is closed-ended. Also make sure you're not pointing yourself towards an answer or solution you already have in mind, such **"How might we better motivate our teams with more money?"** That's prescriptive and has the inherent assumption that money is a motivator (tons of research prove that assumption to be very wrong in many situations).

You question needs to be rephrased as an open-ended question which promotes a fuller, more meaningful answer, such as **"How might we get better engagement from our teams by motivating them more?"**

Another example: **"Can we improve the hospital experience for our patients?"** is closed-ended. Yes we can, or no we can't. To open it up, we'd change it to **"How might we improve the hospital experience for our patients?"**

Higher or Lower Scope.

Morgan D. Jones, the CIA veteran, dives into great detail about problem solving techniques, and I can paraphrase his key point as being that the most common mistakes are mistakes of scope – solving a problem at a level too high or too low.

The go-to technique here is known as The 5 Whys, created by Toyota's Taiichi Ohno. It is well documented online, so no need to reiterate it here. Suffice to say, everyone at Amazon is drilled in this root cause technique, and it is favoured by IDEO and championed by Eric Ries in *The Lean Startup*.

If you're dealing with a technical Problem Focus, it might be a good idea to bring this into Step 1, when you are stating your focus. It's important to aim for the right level from the outset.

Reframing.

Reframing can take a perceived problem and completely tip it on its head, creating a massive creative force field all of its own which drives us to look for and see completely different opportunities and solutions.

Restating our problem broadens our perspective of a problem, according to Morgan Jones, and usually points us towards the fact there is more than one problem and more than one solution.

Thomas Wedell-Wedellsborg, the problem solving specialist, uses the classic case of the problem of the slow elevator. The immediate temptation, he says, is to head for the solution space in which we brainstorm **"How to make the elevator faster?"** All solutions cluster around the assumption that the elevator is too slow. But it may be already technically as fast as possible; perhaps it's suffering from lunch-time peak hour crowds or something else.

So the problem needs to be reframed. Is there another, better, problem to solve?

What if we step back and look at the problem behind the problem, by identifying a different aspect of the problem?

"What's the problem with that problem?" is how I might phrase the reframing question.

"The wait is annoying," is really what needs to be tackled here. So our question might become **"How might we make the wait less annoying?"** or **"How might we make the wait *feel* shorter?"** Suddenly, the solution space fills itself with things like mirrors, playing music, or installing hand sanitizers.

Disney are masters of solving exactly this type of reframed problem. Queues are a fact of life at Disney parks so they ingeniously introduced entertainment and distractions to make the line for that ride seem shorter, and indeed, an entertainment in itself, which builds anticipation. A masterstroke of reframing because you found a better problem to solve.

CISCO was already at the forefront of teleconferencing, but, being the progressive company they are, they didn't rest there. They had the question **"How can we improve teleconferencing?"** in place already. But they kicked into high thinking gear by reframing it as **"How can we provide a viable alternative to air travel?"** Think about that for a moment. Their customers are typically using their systems as a way to avoid jumping on another expensive plane ride. So what will replace or replicate the face-to-face experience? One of my favourite reframing questions of all.

But tech doesn't, nor shouldn't, have a monopoly on reframing questions for a better result. For years, hotdog-eating contests were dominated by large-bodied Americans stuffing their faces, while answering to the best of their ability, the question: **"How do I eat more hotdogs?"**

Then in 2001, the crowd smirked wryly as a slim Japanese guy, Kobayashi-san, weighing just 59kg stepped up to the plate (get it?) at Nathan's Coney Island Hot Dog Eating Contest.

He reframed the problem. His question was **"How do I make hotdogs easier to eat?"** And by unbundling the problem in this way, he worked out you didn't need to eat the bun and the sausage together, and in fact, it all went down way easier if you soaked the buns in water to make them soggy first. Result?

He gobbled his way through 50 hot dogs in 12 minutes, doubling the previous record of 25. He went on to set a world of world record of 110 hotdogs in 10 minutes in 2012 at the New York State Fair. Yes, I feel a little ill, too.

You might well be sipping on a Starbucks coffee as you're reading this. Well, don't choke, because you're about to see how founder Howard Schulz improved his question to take the stand-alone coffee shop from Le Grande Failure, into a global behemoth.

His first guiding question was **"How can I recreate Italian espresso bars in the USA?"** He did this too faithfully. With opera music, and no seats, so everyone was standing around sipping their Joe. Not to Americans' taste. After some customer feedback, the new question became **"How can I create a comfortable, relaxing environment to enjoy great coffee?"** Aha! The third place experience was successfully created.

Many of these fall into the same situation of identifying immediate solutions to the *perceived* problem, whereas challenging what the *real* problem is yields more creative and fruitful results.

Tony Faddell, one of Apple's key designers before founding Nest who sold to Google for $3.2 billion, sums this up nicely. "It's seeing the invisible problem, not just the obvious problem, that's important. There are invisible problems all around us, ones we can solve. But first we need to see them, to feel them."

Reversing.

The poster child for improving a question by reversing is Henry Ford. **"How can I get each team to the car faster?"** was the prevailing thought process in the early days of the motorcar world. Factories converged on trying to improve delivery on that problem.

Along came the visionary Henry Ford, who flipped the question on its head with the reversal technique. **"How can I get the car to the work team faster?"** was the question that set in motion his observation of butcher's hanging racks and other systems that resulted in the assembly line as the more efficient way to move the cars to the men, not the other way round. Production times plunged by 774 % (from 12 hours to just 93 minutes within 4 years) and company value compounded by 43% *per annum* from 1906 to 1920.

Ford was essentially asking **"How might we produce the least expensive car in the world?"**

But again this problem can be restated another way. Along came William Durant, CEO of General Motors, and fine-tuned the question. **"How might we make a car that people could *afford?*"**

His solution was not to make it cheaper than a Model T Ford, but by helping them pay for an even better, more expensive car, using instalment plan financing. GMAC was set up in 1919 and set the wheels in motion for GM to outsell Ford.

Positive and Negative Verbs.

David Kord Murray, former NASA scientist turned author and all-round insightful human being, encourages us to play with the verbs of a question.

Especially experimenting with positive and negative verbs to see if that shakes loose a different angle or insight.

"It's the same essential problem," he says, "but changing the point of view from positive to negative can change the solution it produces."

The example he gives is this:

"How can I improve the efficiency of our workers?" is the problem stated positively because of the word "improve". But, turn that around to "reduce" and the question becomes **"How can I reduce the time spent working on the product?"** and shifts focus to perhaps breaking the task into smaller, more manageable tasks, or even to robotics and AI solutions.

Active or Passive Verbs.

Verbs is where the real aggressive energy of a question lies. Playing with the verb will add some spark, sizzle and pop when you find the right one.

Often paraphrasing your problem can shake it loose a bit, and expose energetic words that shift us towards a new perspective. Or pull out the thesaurus and find similar alternative words for it.

Rather than a straightforward **"How might we reduce the price ...?"** compare **"How might we *shatter* existing price levels ...?"**

"How might we beat competitors ...?" becomes **"How might we *decimate* the competition ...?"**

Feel how these let off the handbrake and excite you to start thinking even bigger?

Switching perspectives.

Instead of seeing everything from your same point of view, or company-out, what if you phrase the question from your customers' perspective, consumer-in?

For example, **"How might we delight our customers?"** becomes **"How might ABC company delight me?"**

"How might we improve our patients' hospital experience?" becomes **"How might my stay in this hospital be a better/safer/more enjoyable experience?"** Once again, playing with variables shapes the problem you're trying to find.

Broader or More Specific.

If there's a word like "people" in your question, it's probably too broad. For example, **"How might we sell more widgets to people?"**

What kind of people? Are they Millennials? Retirees? Double Income No Kids people? Get more specific.

Similarly if your question is "**How might we sell more widgets in Singapore?**" you might consider widening the scope to "**How might we sell more widgets in Southeast Asia?**" or even wider to "**How might we sell more widgets in Asia?**"

Changing the aperture from rifle to shotgun (or vice versa) sets in motion a different opportunity. You should feel it viscerally.

Pulling things apart.

A stand-by of problem solving is always to see if the problem can be broken down further into smaller, more manageable chunks.

"If you can't solve a problem, then there is an easier problem to solve. Find it," advises George Polya, former Hungarian mathematician and Stanford professor.

So, can parts of your question be pulled out from the whole?

By zeroing in, does this give a particular focus or emphasis which is more fertile now that it has been exposed?

In a familiar tale, a few young guys had a location sharing app start-up, called Urbn. They were answering the question: "**How can we create a great location sharing app?**" It failed. But amid the wreckage, they noticed that users seemed to be really gung-ho about one specific feature of the app: photo sharing. So a new question was asked: "**How can we create a simple photo sharing app?**"The answer to that zoom-in pivot was Instagram, with an estimated 300,000,000 active users and a value of $35 billion!

Or let's take Keller Rinaudo's question about his drones in Africa: "**How can we ensure that our Zip drones** arrive safely at its destination, using more affordable components, at a smaller scale so it can service cases where lives are at risk?"

There's a question begging to be attacked and broken down into bite-sized pieces for greater clarity, focus and priority.

Why don't you try to help him out now – sharpen that question by focusing on one or perhaps two elements only, and making it a really actionable question.

KILLER QUESTION ADVANCED FORMULA.

So you're feeling chuffed that you've got your How Might We Killer Question, and subjected it to several rounds of improvement.

Here's a more advanced way you might like to try and phrase your question for greater comprehensiveness:

"HOW MIGHT WE (ACTION) OUR (OBJECT) MORE (QUALIFIER) SO PEOPLE WILL (END RESULT)?"

The Action is the thing you want to do/change. Think verbs.

The Object is the item or person you want to change.

The Qualifier is the type of action or change you want.

The End Result is the outcome (quantitative or qualitative) you want or expect.

So, to take our earlier pharmaceutical R&D situation, that might become:

"How might we (get) our (drugs approved) more (quickly) so people will (begin enjoying better health sooner)?"

Zipline's question **"How can we ensure that our Zip drones arrive safely at its destination, using more affordable components, at a smaller scale so it can service cases where lives are at risk?"** could be shoehorned into this format.

"How might we ensure that our Zip drones arrive more safely at their destination so villagers' lives will be less at risk?"

Your first few attempts might come out a bit clumsy but remain fluid in the process. It doesn't have to map grammatically exactly, as long as you are ticking the main boxes in the format.

ADVANCED TECHNIQUE: 180-DEGREE WRONG THINKING.

Let's finish on a big fat fun disruptive technique here ...

This advanced technique is a close relative of reversing, but I think of it more as flip-flopping, like a fish you've just hooked and landed on the deck of your boat. It's thrashing around, flipping, flopping and flapping like mad.

So instead of saying **"How can we reduce employee absenteeism?"** reframe it as **"How can we encourage employees to stay away from work?"** By understanding the opposite problem, and ideating on it, we can generate better framing and solutions for the actual problem we want to solve.

This step can involve a whole new round of assumption challenging: **"What are we *really* trying to do here?"** as Pierre Omidyar would say. Or, **"Why do we need this?"** as Orit Gadeish, former CEO of Bain loved asking.

I've done this sort of exercise with Accor, where one of their German hotel GMs threw his hands up in the air: "Agh, this pointless. What is the value of brainstorming for the worst possible hotel experience? We are luxury hotels!"

I explained that if we have insights and ideas as to what might make the worst experience, we can flip those 180-degrees to inspire thinking directions into what might constitute the best. "*Ohhh*!"

Same with Solvay the chemical company, who were responsible for 60% of the components of the Solar Impulse 2 record-breaking round-the-world flight. **"How can we design a solar plane that could not fly?"** was the assignment I set them. One of the solutions was to make it out of house bricks, which, when flipped, led to further explorations of the lightest possible materials.

Fun, fertile and fruitful possibilities usually erupt.

YOUR KILLER QUESTION

S o this is it, folks. It's what's emerged from your Killer Question pipeline.

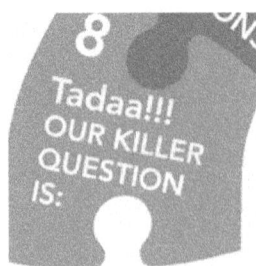

OUR KILLER QUESTION IS ...

"
....
...."

It's fun to go back and see where the inflection points were, such as which basic assumption did this insight originally spring from?

Hopefully your Killer Question above is fizzing with energy and insight and possibility.

Hopefully it's already got you and your team buzzed because it's created a cognitive gap that you're just dying to close.

Hopefully you're foaming at the mouth to get to work and solve it.

How to "brainstorm" the solutions is outside the scope of this book, but it's not outside the scope of my work. Perhaps I'll tackle that topic in my next book.

Now the best thing to do is pin up your Killer Question on your wall for you and all to see, to invite different perspectives into your solution world.

One of my innovation gurus, Hal Gregersen, now director at the MIT Leadership Center, advises we spend 5 minutes each day for 2-4 weeks trying to improve the question and mull it over. Set a timeline to come back and ideate the solutions.

Who knows who drops by and might just have an explosive insight and shoot out the lights with an answer to your question. Because it's not just about you, the lone creative genius, it's about *we*.

"How might *we* come up with an explosive solution to our Killer Question?"

Before leaving the office for the day is a good time to review the question, or before bedtime even better. Leave the subconscious to weave it's magic of associative thinking. Because as Prof David Cooperrider, from the Drucker School of Management, says: "A powerful question never sleeps."

I sincerely trust you've found this ride inspiring and mind-opening, and it's lit your creative fuse. So, what are YOUR questions? Let me know any good questions you've seen, read, heard about, or even generated yourself to help create explosive solutions.

Fire in the hole!

STU'S KILLER QUESTION STOCKPILE

I am a compulsive capturer, and I urge you to become one too if you're not already. I use Notes app on my iPhone to capture everything – 'to do' lists, research for my books, music and movie suggestions from friends, etc.

Robert Epstein PhD, the man behind *Psychology Today* magazine, maintains that if you master Capturing skills your creative output will skyrocket by up to 90%.

Richard Branson is a great example of a great capturer, keeping a notebook full of questions that occur to him.

So, now I'm going to share and set free a selection of random questions from my own private Killer Questions list. Who knows, there might be a line of questioning in there that sparks a game-changing idea in you. Or at very least, it will give you a glimpse into the dark and mysterious world that is my fevered Creative, Curious and Crazy mind at work (and play).

Feel free to play around with these, and workshop them by taking them through the system from Why to What if to How to get the hang of it, and maybe strike some inspiration.

MY WHY? QUESTIONS:
Why is mental health so fragile among creative types?

Why is there so much physical violence in Australia, UK, USA, etc?

Why do Muslims create disturbance once they reach a certain percentage of population in a country?

Why is world peace so hard to achieve?

Why do so many entertainers commit suicide?

Why do so many "successful" people commit suicide?

Why do kangaroos box?

Why are olden times more romantic?

Why does it take 4-5 people in emerging countries to do the job of 1 in a developed place?

Why is bass guitar such a primal thing? And how can we make the ukelele more primal?

Why have we (Westerners) become such a casual society?

Why is it that people from collectivist cultures can be so obliviously selfish?

Why don't we know much about Elon Musk even though he's arguably the best living thinker? (And, despite being that, follows me on Twitter.)

Why do we always smile/grin when we just make it safely across the road?

Why are universities so cumbersome and bureaucratic?

Why can't we make an invisible microphone?

Why does such a small percentage of aid money and resources reach those on the ground who need it? Is there a way to cut out the middle-man?

Why does music resonate with handicapped people so much?

Why do people want to follow fashion and wear the same thing as others?

Why is it so hard for most people to earn a living?

Why do Westerners dress so casually and poorly compared to Asians?

Why is it that those with the least to say seem to say it the loudest?

Why is there so much dissatisfaction when I check into hotels?

Why don't most online hotel booking sites have addresses and phone numbers in local language so the taxi driver knows where to go?

Why do poor people speak louder than rich people? And with such harshly angular accents?

Why are emerging countries less safety conscious than developed countries?

Why can't I run a webinar without having an expensive contractual arrangement?

Why do we have to work so hard just to survive? Is there another way to run life?

Why is it that high-earning successful people can become unsuccessful? And eventually end up wiping arses in nursing homes for a living, and/or committing suicide?

Why is it that the more we earn the more we spend? How can we be successful without ramping up the outgoings, overheads, and expenses?

Why do the good die young?

Why are Filipinos such good singers and musicians?

Why do I often feel so poor even though I'm probably in the top 3-5% of the world?

Why do we need to be monogamous?

Why do Africans and Latin Americans have such an innate sense of rhythm?

Why is Hong Kong the only place in the world where taxis have an auto door opening mechanism?

Why do fat people often seem friendlier?

Why do chefs wear big white hats and checkered pants?

Why do butchers wear blue and white stripes?

Why are there only two sides of politics?

MY WHAT IF? QUESTIONS:
What if the sun exploded?
What if a training company were run like a health club?
What if this change represents an opportunity for us?
What if I asked more What if questions???

MY HOW? QUESTIONS.
How can we make lack of creativity a problem worth solving?
How can we make a drink that's more refreshing than beer?
How might we feed 7 billion people better?
How can we improve mental health in modern urban life?
How can I create 100,000 innovation dynamos?
How come the leapfrog effect works or kicks into action?
How come many girls in communist countries can often be and act way more sexy than their capitalist counterparts?
How can music speak so deeply to us?
How can I play the ukulele not like a ukulele?
How could we better avoid burnout?
How might we create a ukelele craze in China?
How can we drink beer and not get fat?
How might we prevent and protect ourselves against lung cancer in cities with filthy air quality?

What are YOUR Killer Questions? Let me know great questions you've seen, heard, read about or asked. I'd love to hear (and share) them at stu@hotheads-innovation.com

BIBLIOGRAPHY, WEBLIOGRAPHY, VIDEOGRAPHY.

Books, magazines, newspapers.

A More Beautiful Question. The Power of Inquiry to Spark Breakthrough Ideas. Warren Berger.

Borrowing Brilliance. The Six Steps to Business Innovation by Building on the Ideas of Others. David Kord Murray.

Crazy is a Compliment. The Power of Zigging when Everyone else is Zagging. Linda Rottenberg.

Fast Company magazine. July/August 2016.

Financial Times. Stranger Things Happen. 23/24 September 2017.

Firms of Endearment. How World Class Companies Profit from Passion and Purpose. Rajendra Sisodia, David Wolfe, Jagdish N. Sheth.

Gretzky. An Autobiography. Wayne Gretzky.

Harvard Business Review, October 2015. On Making Carrots Cool. Jeffrey Dunn.

Hit Makers. The Science of Popularity in an Age of Distraction. Derek Thompson.

How to Solve It. A New Aspect of Mathematical Method. George Polya.

It's Not About the Shark. David Niven.

Jugaad Innovation. A Frugal and Flexible approach to

Innovation for the 21st Century. Navi Radjou, Jaideep Prabhu, Simone Ahuja.

Lead with a Story. A Guide to Crafting Business Narratives that Captivate, Convince and Inspire. Paul Smith.

Lovemarks. The Future Beyond Brands. Kevin Roberts.

Made to Stick. Why Some Ideas Survive and Others Die. Chip Heath & Dan Heath.

Mavericks at Work. Why the most original minds in business win. William Taylor and Polly LaBarre.

Meaningful. The Story of Ideas that Fly. Bernadette Jiwa.

Pre-Suasion. A Revolutionary Way to Influence and Persuade. Robert Cialdini.

Red Teaming. How Your Business Can Conquer the Competition by Challenging Everything. Bryce G Hoffman.

Rejection Proof. How to Beat Fear and Become Invincible. Jia Jiang.

Rethink. The Surprising History of Ideas. Steven Poole.

Simplify. How the Best Businesses in the World Succeed. Richard Koch & Greg Lockwood.

Sydney Morning Herald newspaper. Various editions, 2016-8.

TED Talks. The Official TED Guide to Public Speaking. Chris Anderson.

The Art of Creative Thinking. Rod Judkins.

The Medici Effect. What Elephants & Epidemics Can Teach us About Innovation. Frans Johansson.

The Thinker's Toolkit. 14 Powerful Techniques for Problem Solving. Morgan D Jones.

The Three Box Solution. A Strategy for Leading Innovation. Vijay Govindarajan.

The Tipping Point. How Little Things Can Make a Big Difference. Malcolm Gladwell.

Think Like a Freak. Steven D Levitt and Stephen J. Dubner.
Visual Intelligence. Sharpen Your Perception, Change Your Life. Amy E Herman.
Win Your Case. How to Present, Persuade, and Prevail – Every Place, Every Time. Gerry Spence.
Zero to One. Notes on Startups, or How to Build the Future. Peter Thiel.
Zig Zag. The Surprising Path to Greater Creativity. Keith Sawyer.

Websites.
Amazon.com
Basadur.com
C2melbourne.com
Cool.haus
Endeavor.org
FastCompany.com: *How Willow Creek is Leading Evangelicals by Learning from the Business World*
Feliciayap.com
Goop.com
Halgregersen.com
HBR.org: *I joined AirBnb at 52 and Here's what I learned about Age, Wisdom and the Tech Industy.* Chip Conley.
Lumiar.org.br
Noushouse.co
Psyblog.com
Razerzone.com
Redhongyi.com
Rightquestion.org
Santafe.edu
Shortyawards.com *Naked Juice Power Garden*
Socklady.com
Umamiburger.com
Wired.com

Videos.

In the Future, even Broccoli will Have an IP Address. Caleb Harper. Wired video.

Khanacademy.org *Pixar in a Box*

The Russell Howard Hour

TED.com

Designers – Think Big! Tim Brown.

From Mach-2 Glider to Hummingbird Drone. Regina Dugan.

How to run a company with (almost) no rules. Ricardo Semler.

I'm sure there were other sources that may have been inadvertently omitted or lost to time. Please accept our apologies and advise us if so.

TRAIN YOUR TEAM IN KILLER QUESTIONS TECHNIQUES

Did you know that creativity is up to 80% learned and acquired? Yes, we can ALL learn, practice and develop creativity, considered the #1 required leadership skill in the 21st century.

At Hotheads, we offer in-house training, motivational keynotes, and ideation facilitation by Stu Lloyd, Asia Pacific's most in-demand business creativity training expert. So if your team needs turbo-charging to Find the Future with more explosive creative thinking skills, contact us today.

Work with Stu: stu@hotheads-innovation.com

See more at Hotheads Innovation website

hotheads
EXPLOSIVE THINKING
www.hotheads-innovation.com

KILLER QUESTIONS IN-HOUSE TRAINING.

How to Ask Better Questions to Create Breakthrough Solutions.

Imagine upskilling your team with this impactful, powerful and explosive tool, considered a core competency in the New Economy.

Suitable for every type of business from start-ups to Fortune 500s.

This one-of-a-kind program experience, designed and delivered personally by Stu Lloyd, is available exclusively from Hotheads.

All attendees will receive a copy of **Killer Questions**, signed by Stu.

Other Creativity/Innovation Skills Programs:
- **POP THINK: 4 Core Creative Competencies**
- **INNOV8TOR: 5 Innovation Discovery Skills**
- **3 Thinking Traps (and how to Escape them)**
- **Thinking on Your Feet: Fast & Flexible Improvisational Thinking Skills**
- **Extreme Ideation & Brainstorm, and Harvesting Skills**
- **Visual Perception Skills for Front-line Professionals**
- **BIG T Thinking – Thinking, Deep and Wide**

IS THERE A KILLER QUESTIONS ONLINE TRAINING PROGRAM?

S tu got to thinking: "How can I reach audiences and deliver my valuable material and messages beyond Fortune 500s in Asia Pacific without jumping on a plane?"

The answer:

HOTHEADHACKS.MYKAJABI.COM

So, YES! Now for the first time, creatives anywhere in the world can access Stu's blogs, trainings, and video materials *online*, in your own time zone, from the comfort of our your office (or even in your underwear on the sofa if that's how you roll).

(We are progressively building out the Hothead Hacks Future Skills online training programs, and **Killer Questions** will be the first to be uploaded when ready.)

Sign up for free and join the global **Hothead Hacks Creative Community** today to get regular free doses of explosive inspiration direct from Stu.

hotheadhacks
FUTURE SKILLS SERIES >>

WHAT THE HELL IS CATMATDOG?

Did you know that 70% of all purchase decisions are made on an emotional basis, not a rational basis? Because people don't buy facts, they buy feelings.

At CATMATDOG, we are Asia's most in-demand executive communication experts delivering Strategic Storytelling, Persuasive Presentation Skills, and Pitch Coaching.

So if you or your team needs help to unleash your skills to Captivate, Convince and Convert better, get in touch with Stu today.

topdog@catmatdog.com

CHECK OUT CATMATDOG.COM FOR OUR FULL STORY.

CAT MAT DOG

STRATEGIC STORYTELLING ★ PRESENTATION PSYCHOLOGY ★ PITCH COACHING

As Chris Anderson, Head of *TED*, said:

"In the 21st Century there's a new superpower ... it's called presentation literacy. The good news is these skills are absolutely teachable."

In-house training programs designed and delivered by Stu Lloyd:

- **Explosive Business Storytelling Skills for Managers**
- **StorySelling for Sales/Marketing Teams**
- **StoryLiving (corporate values-based story development)**
- **StoryLeading for Managers and CEOs**
- **Pitch2Persuade (persuasive presentation psychology)**
- **How to Present Ideas (in a Multinational Environment)**
- **Media Skills for Modern Managers**
- **BOOM! BANG! POW! Digital Content Creation**

A FEW SURPRISES
ABOUT @REALSTULLOYD

S tu is proud of being a 4th generation Zimbabwean, and enjoyed an idyllic childhood growing up in Africa. Feel free to ask Stu about the 65 countries he's visited since, his passion for motorcycle touring, rugby, or world music …

A veritable 'slash guy' renaissance man, Stu Lloyd has been an Advertising Creative Director/ TEDx MC and Speaker Coach/ Best-selling Author / Keynote Speaker and Conference Chairman/ Military History Tour Guide/ Warner Music Songwriter/ Radio Broadcaster/ and more.

Having studied a double-major in Psychology and Mass Communications, Stu has a strong intuitive feel for what makes people tick. And the science of persuasion is one of his personal passions …

In 30 years at the intersection of creativity and commerce, he has successfully pitched and won hundreds of millions of dollars worth of business from clients such as **Adidas, Microsoft, HSBC, Christian Dior, Porsche, New Zealand Tourism, Hilton Asia Pacific, Gatorade, Seagate, Mazda, Tiger Beer**, etc.

During that time he won a number of awards for his persuasive copywriting of TV, radio and print materials. He sold his $20 million advertising agency in Singapore to **DraftFCB**, one of the 'big boy' listed multinational USA networks to pursue his passions.

Stu has since published 8 non-fiction books, and sold in excess of 100,000 copies of his books. See www.stulloyd.com

As **MC for the TEDx event** 'Creativity & Collaboration' in 2011, Stu was also the appointed **speaker coach for all speakers**, and remains active in the TEDx movement as an advisor/coach.

An accomplished speaker and presenter, he's addressed a **United Nations WTO** Conference in China, and chaired/keynoted/MC'd hundreds of conferences in all parts of Asia including as **Chairman of the Chief Innovation Officer Summit, Shanghai 2016, and the Asia Innovation Summit, Jakarta 2017.**

The **Telegraph newspaper, UK, has called him: "The Perfect Storyteller."**

Follow Stu on twitter and instagram: @RealStuLloyd
Connect with Stu on LinkedIn: Stu Lloyd Storyteller

See more on Stu's writing and his upcoming books at
WWW.STULLOYD.COM
Like Stu's Facebook page to be updated on his new ideas and writing
FACEBOOK.COM/STULLOYDSTORYTELLING

OTHER BOOKS BY STU LLOYD

Thinking, Deep and Wide – BIG T: the Thinking Style That's Rocking the New Economy (coming 2019)

Hardship Posting:
True Tales of Expat Misadventure in Asia, Vol 1.

Hardship Posting:
True Tales of Expat Misadventure in Asia, Vol 2.

Hardship Posting:
True Tales of Expat Misadventure in Asia, Vol 3.

Hardship Posting:
True Tales of Expat Misadventure in Asia, Vol 5.

Gone Troppo!:
My Search for Tropical Paradise.

Hare of the Dog:
History, Humour and Hell-raising from the Hash House Harriers.

The Missing Years.
A PoW's Diary from Changi to Hellfire Pass.

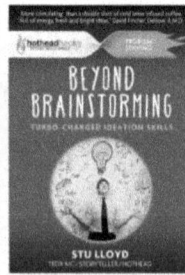

www.ingramcontent.com/pod-product-compliance
Lightning Source LLC
Chambersburg PA
CBHW021940190326
41519CB00009B/1080